THE MOST VALUABLE ADVICE MONEY *CAN'T* BUY

"Anyone who plans to open a restaurant needs a good location, matched with the right merchandising format, the patience of a saint, the resourcefulness of a one-armed magician, the luck of a first-time gambler and a good map indicating roads which may lead you to a town called *Success*. I think you will find *The Complete Restaurateur* just such a map."

—George Lang, proprietor,
Café des Artistes, New York City

Stocked with advice from the successful owners of some of America's most busy bistros, *The Complete Restaurateur* offers guidance on all the challenges that lie between opening day and your dazzling future.

EMPLOYEE RELATIONS
"Everybody sees that it's not beneath me to clear a table, clean it and set it."
—Joe Beyer, owner, Pontchartrain Wine Celler, Detroit

MOTIVATION
"When people leave the restaurant and every one of them says, 'We had such a wonderful time . . .' it inspires you. And you just want to keep going."

—Terry Moore, owner, The Old Mill,
South Egremont, Massachusetts

HOW TO TELL IF THE RESTAURANT BUSINESS IS IN YOUR BLOOD
"No matter how awful an experience you've had, if an opportunity comes up again, you're ready to go."

—Diane Selby, owner, Hail Columbia,
Chatham, New York

Elizabeth Lawrence specializes in writing about food, entertaining, and the food business. Her previous books include *The Complete Caterer* and *The Lenox Book of Home Entertaining and Etiquette*.

W9-CKZ-654

Other Books by Elizabeth Lawrence

The Complete Caterer

*The Lenox Book of Home Entertaining
and Etiquette*

T·H·E
COMPLETE
RESTAURATEUR

A Practical Guide to the Craft and Business of Restaurant Ownership

Elizabeth Lawrence

A PLUME BOOK

PLUME
Published by the Penguin Group
Penguin Books USA Inc., 375 Hudson Street,
New York, New York 10014, U.S.A.
Penguin Books Ltd, 27 Wrights Lane,
London W8 5TZ, England
Penguin Books Australia Ltd, Ringwood,
Victoria, Australia
Penguin Books Canada Ltd, 10 Alcorn Ave.
Toronto, Ontario, Canada M4V 3B2
Penguin Books (N.Z.) Ltd, 182–190 Wairau Road,
Auckland 10, New Zealand

Penguin Books Ltd, Registered Offices:
Harmondsworth, Middlesex, England

First published by Plume, an imprint of New American
Library, a division of Penguin Books USA Inc.

First Printing, January, 1992
10 9 8

 REGISTERED TRADEMARK—MARCA REGISTRADA

LIBRARY OF CONGRESS CATALOGING-IN-PUBLICATION DATA:

Lawrence, Elizabeth.
The complete restaurateur : a practical guide to the craft and
business of restaurant ownership / Elizabeth Lawrence.
p.   cm.
ISBN 0-452-26752-8
1. Restaurant management. I. Title.
TX911.3.M27L42 1992
647.95′068—dc20   91-773
                                                                        CIP

Printed in the United States of America
Set in Century Schoolbook
Designed by Leonard Telesca

It's a wonderful business to be in. . . . When people leave the restaurant and every one of them says "We had such a wonderful time—the food was delicious, the service was great," it inspires you.

And you just want to keep going. You think, "Let's stay open all night. Let's get more people in here!"

—Terry Moore, proprietor of
the Old Mill in South
Egremont, Massachusetts

Contents

CHAPTER

1

The Role of the Restaurateur

An adventurous approach to food and eating has become commonplace in America in the last dozen or so years. Millions of us read food magazines and watch Julia Child and Madeleine Kamman and Justin Wilson on television. We pay attention, we care, and we know what we like.

One result of this raised food consciousness is that everybody has opinions about the food they buy. This new level of expertise reaches into the sphere of the restaurant industry, too, as even casual diners pay attention to service, presentation, and the freshness of ingredients. This has produced a broadened base for the restaurant business itself.

The lure of restaurateurship can be very strong. I would be willing to bet that almost anyone who loves food and eating out muses at one time or another about opening their own place. Like you, for example.

A Business for Everybody?

How often do you think of opening your own restaurant? Do you find that every time you go out to eat you mentally compare the restaurant to others you've liked—and perhaps to the one you've created for yourself in your mind? Perhaps you have found that having worked in someone else's restaurant for years, you now have absolute confidence that you could do it better.

You may even have looked around your area and observed a positive need for a restaurant different from those that already exist. Do you think to yourself every time you eat out, "I think I could make a success of it. I know I can do it just as well as The Chat and Chew. Possibly I can do it a great deal better. Maybe I just will."

If you've thought a lot about running your own restaurant, you probably have a concept in mind and a vision of the sort of experience you will provide. You may have worked out in your mind what the dining experience will be like—that may be what you know best. You may have confidence in your business sense and be ready to give it a try.

Successful people from all professions—accountants, lawyers, doctors, bankers, business people—are opening restaurants. If you poll people who are considering opening a restaurant about their qualifications, many will jokingly say, "Well, I eat out a lot." And for some people, that's all it takes to kindle an interest in running a restaurant, a simple desire born of eating out and loving food.

This kind of "experience"—that is, eating out often and enjoyably—can be invaluable. Before you abandon your posture as a customer, imprint upon your memory—now and forever—the basic demands you have of the commercial establishments in which you dine.

This means, for example, you must think through every single aspect of your restaurant. How would you respond as a new customer to orange wallpaper or booming speakers?

Remember, too, that the performance your eventual customers experience must be one that *they* want to see. When you go to a play or a movie that challenges you to think, you may find it worthwhile even though it isn't necessarily fun. In contrast, however, you as a diner don't want to be challenged in a restaurant. If you wouldn't like it, your customers probably wouldn't either, so be careful about pushing or lecturing your patrons in food selection or in your manner of serving them. If you do, chances are that some of those patrons will never return.

Imagine your own experience and translate your responses as a customer into what you do as a restaurateur.

Success in another field does not necessarily translate into success in the restaurant industry. In many ways, running a food service establishment is different from other businesses, from the accounting methods used to techniques of personnel management. Unfortunately, the individuality of the restaurant business, which is surely part of its appeal, is something that few people understand when they first start out.

New York–based restaurant consultant Gary Goldberg says, "Just because someone is smart, or street smart, or has made a career success in another area, it does not automatically translate into the restaurant business. There is so much to know that no one can learn it all. Although you can learn enough to know when you need help and how to get it."

The intelligent restaurateur uses his or her own tastes and experiences. But a key lesson is the realization that while you may think you are an expert—and you may well be in certain areas of running a restaurant—you probably have a good deal yet to learn. That's true even of people who have been in the restaurant business for years—as they will be the first to tell you.

Welcome to the Show. . . .

We all love to be entertained—and coddled—when we go out to eat. A trip to a restaurant takes us out of our eat-at-home rituals and exposes us to something potentially exciting or even exotic. This escape-from-the-normal quality is true for the humblest breakfast diner, the poshest of French restaurants, and everything in between.

You just don't get the same show-business quality in your dining room. And, of course, back home you'd also have to do the dishes.

The experience of eating in a restaurant is akin to that of going to the theater. The action around you transpires for your benefit, to satisfy your wants and needs. There's an inherent excitement, an energy, a sought-after surprise to the best restaurant experiences. Indeed, the sense of escape from the humdrum of everyday life is one of the main reasons most of us go out to eat.

In many cases, it is also the explanation of why many of us decide we want to become restaurateurs ourselves.

A useful mind-set for the aspiring restaurateur, in fact, is to regard your theoretical eating establishment as a kind of theatrical environment, one that has been carefully designed for the entertainment of your customers. As Diane Selby, co-owner with her husband, Donald, of Hail Columbia in Chatham, New York, told me, "You have to create a stage set. You have to have a good stage manager, good lighting, colors, actors—the whole thing must work together."

Once your customers arrive, you must make them feel at all times as if, individually and collectively, they are at center stage. The decor must establish a particular atmosphere, the waiting staff must perform their assigned roles (unobtrusively, one hopes), and the food must please each diner's eye and palate.

The need for a certain theatricality sets running a restaurant apart from most other businesses. People don't go to a dentist or a lawyer or a retail establishment with the same attitude they have when they arrive at the door of your restaurant. They come to eat on your premises because they expect to have a good time there. They want to be fed, of course, but they also want to leave savoring the experience of the meal you just served.

Terry Moore, co-owner with his wife, Juliet, of the Old Mill in South Egremont, Massachusetts, and The White Hart in Salisbury, Connecticut, summarizes his view of the restaurateur's task this way: "We're here for you to come in for the next two hours and to have a wonderful time. Everybody's got problems. But once you step inside these doors, they're forgotten."

To carry the theatrical metaphor one step further, eating in restaurants is akin to participatory theater. The customer is forever evaluating, scrutinizing the food, the service, and the decor. Equally subject to assessment are the lighting, staff uniforms, the menus, rest rooms—in short, everything in the restaurant. Yet in the best-run restaurants the diner is blithely unaware of most of the elements. The experience is seamless.

On the other hand, in the instances when the elements don't work perfectly, the diner notices, and it influences the decision to return.

It's a bit like going to a really good show. Most of us are largely inarticulate afterward about the experience. We say it was wonderful or moving or lots of fun. But after a bad show? If you're being nice, you come out saying something like, "Well, at least the dancing was great." More likely, you're asking your companions why those people bothered or you're murmuring about the ticket prices or offering up a hundred other little complaints about why the show left you disappointed.

Restaurants are the same: if the total experience works, if all the elements blend to make it wonderful, there's a feeling of satisfaction. The best restaurateur aims to achieve an overall sense of pleasurable escape.

What Makes a Good Restaurant?

There's no one simple answer to that question. But there are some useful ways of considering the answers.

A restaurant is the sum of its parts, and every part is distinct and important. Like the conductor surveying a temperamental orchestra, the good restaurateur combines and balances the elements into a cohesive "orchestrated" whole.

A number of the people who talked to me observed, in one

way or another, that the restaurant business is really all about details. They concluded, therefore, that the better you manage those details, the better your restaurant will be.

To put it another way, you can't afford to think for a moment that your goals can be limited to having good or even great food. It is an unwritten rule in the business that the best food in the world is no guarantee of success.

In the same way, a good location, a pretty space, and attentive service are valuable and important; taken individually none of them will guarantee anything. To have a good restaurant you need to combine all of them: the place must be attractive, the food tasty, and the service pleasant (which means the workers must be able to get along with one another as well as with the customers). The pricing, too, must seem reasonable to your patrons.

Terry Moore put it well when he said, "We're satisfying so many of the senses. The sense of taste, the sense of smell, the sense of sight, the feel, the sound. All of these things combine to make a restaurant. So you may be a great chef, but if you don't know what's going on out front, or if you don't really know how to satisfy people's senses, it doesn't all work."

Making all the pieces work together is a key component of making a restaurant work.

There's another way to address the question, What makes a good restaurant? Stated simply, your goal should be to create the best restaurant of its kind, whatever or wherever it may be. You need not serve elaborate meals or the newest of the new. Your dining room needn't be the biggest around, nor your menu the most varied. But you should aim high in creating the best restaurant you know how.

That it be a product of your thinking is also important. A good restaurant is a product of its owner's skill, imagination, and taste. Every good one has intangible qualities that distinguish it, qualities that are often reflections of its proprietor's personality.

In the words of George Lang, restaurant consultant and owner of Café des Artistes in New York, "Whatever you can do as a restaurateur to create an identity is a step in the right direction."

Most successful restaurants seem to reflect the owner's style. According to Gary Goldberg, "One thing I've learned as a consultant over many years is that the personal style of the restaurateur is vitally important. If I go in as a consultant and set up an operation and get everything blended beautifully so that there is one clear image, it won't hold together if the restaurateur has a different style."

Many of us, on examining most franchise restaurants, would automatically conclude that one is much the same as any other. But it's simply not true. Examining an exceptional case, in fact, offers an illuminating insight into how a certain character can individualize and enhance the dining experience. Even seemingly ownerless restaurants such as franchise outlets reflect the chosen style of their overall management as well as the personalities and abilities of the people running them.

Some franchises work while others fail, and it isn't always a matter of location. No doubt you've visited a McDonald's, a Taco Bell, or some other fast-food joint where the service was bad, the cashiers were rude, the food slow in coming, or the lettuce brown and wilted. And you've been in others where the lines moved rapidly, the food arrived on time and just cooked, the rest rooms were meticulously kept, and the staff pleasant. Again, at the good and bad eateries, everything is dependent on the manager or owner.

Some franchise outlets manage to present surprisingly distinct personalities. One McDonald's, located in New York City's financial district, features fresh flowers on the tables and in the rest rooms, complimentary grapes and strawberries on the breakfast menu, and cappucino and French pastries from one of the city's premier bakeries in the afternoon. A uniformed doorman ushers customers in, while a customer-service manager oversees fourteen hostesses dressed in purple and fuschia uniforms who direct patrons to empty tables, hand around napkins, straws, and forgotten condiments. Live piano music is provided throughout the day by a staff of three musicians who perform on a catwalk high above the patrons. All of this is the vision of Frank Madalone, the owner, who has seven other franchises in the city.

Whether your culinary symbol is to be a wally-burger or a beef Wellington, you would do well to consider your own sense of quality: Your place should be a reflection of your personality, tastes, and culinary aspirations.

Excuse Me, Is This Easy Street?

For many people, the notion of opening a restaurant seems like the fast track to Easy Street. You get to eat out every night. Better yet, you get to eat out and drink for free. You can entertain friends without having to do the work. Plus, you choose your hours, taking time off whenever you want.

The picture only gets better over time. When your restaurant takes off people will clamor to get in, making it one of the hot spots in town. You will become something of a celebrity. Your rewards will be acclaim, an easy lifestyle, and a king's ransom in profits.

All dreams must come to an end, so let's terminate this soft-focus fantasy. The realities of opening a restaurant are vastly different than this unlikely little vignette.

Yes, it is true you, as the restaurateur, will get to eat out every night. But that's because when you run a restaurant you're never home. Most restaurateurs and chefs, in fact, come to savor the brief time each week they get to spend with their families. Many come to regret the fact that their children grow up before they have a chance to know them. Unless the restaurant closes down for a specific period each year (such as in areas where the business is seasonal or in a city where expense-account restaurants close for a few weeks in the summer), there are no vacations for those in charge, at least for the first few years while the restaurant becomes established. So much for taking time off.

Yes, you get to eat and drink for free. Consider, however, that you'll be eating a constant diet of your restaurant's food, up to three meals a day. You won't be going out to other restaurants anymore—forget about that—you need to be working at your own. After all, you'll probably be there from the morning (or if you're open for breakfast, from the middle of the night) until well after closing time. You'll be working while your friends socialize. And if you're working, you won't be able to have a constant round of wine or cocktails. That is, if you want to stay in business.

You may not pay directly for your food and drink, but you do pay indirectly, and you work damn hard for them.

For many of us the notion of being able to eat our main meals in a first quality restaurant sounds like paradise. However, if you've spent your whole day, every day, around the food, often the last thing you really want is to eat it for your meals. Robert Del Grande, chef and owner with his wife, Mimi, of the popular Café Annie and Café Express in Houston, says they rarely eat from their menu: "Usually, if you cook it all the time, you get saturated." So it's not uncommon to find a pizza delivery van outside the restaurant around five in the evening. Alison Price, owner of Alison on Dominick in New York, another chic and popular restaurant, reports that when they are too busy to cook a staff meal or "are sick of our food," they have burritos brought in.

You get to choose your hours, all right—as long as they coincide with the restaurant's hours. As the one in charge you are responsible for the operations of the restaurant, from the ordering of the food, to its preparation, service, and cleanup. This remains true even if you have a manager and a large staff.

You are also responsible for all finances, day-to-day and long-term. If the sinks back up, you are the one who must cope with getting them fixed. If the meat delivery is late, you will be on the phone frantically searching for suitable substitutes. You may not chop the vegetables (although if yours is a very small establishment, you may well be doing that, too), but all responsibility for the success or failure of your restaurant falls to you. There is rarely time off, at least in the beginning. Whatever you need in the way of free time must be squeezed from the needs of the restaurant and the staff you employ. And there are the constant worries about meeting payroll and paying the rent and those cash-only suppliers.

For the really bad news, thousands of restaurants open

each year and, sadly, many of them fail. In fact, a restaurant is one of the most risky businesses to start. According to the New York State Restaurant Association, 75 percent of all restaurants in the state fail or change hands within five years of opening. That's a frightening figure, but you have to remember that a restaurant is a small business and that small businesses are risky by definition.

On the upside, if you plan well, work hard, and get really lucky, you may become the hottest joint in town. But then, of course, you have got to work to stay that way, constantly keeping up with trends and a fickle clientele.

Now for Some Good News . . .

Okay, so Easy Street isn't so easy to find. But you're still interested in opening a restaurant? Let's look at the bright side.

While operating a restaurant is a lot of hard work, there are rewards. If it's a business suited to you and your needs, the psychic and financial rewards can be great.

People who have opened their own restaurants report that for many it gets to be second nature. George Lang, owner of Café des Artistes in Manhattan, likens it to a malady: "We Hungarians have a national disease known as restaurantitis, and I am one of its sufferers." But he says it with pride and aplomb, his backdrop a world-famous and widely admired eatery.

For some people, it seems to be genetic. Paulette and Kenny Merlino, a brother-and-sister team who opened Hot Diggity, a hot-dog restaurant, and then Hot Diggity Bar and Grill, both in New York City, figure it's in their blood, as they represent the third generation in the business and are grandchildren of "the hot-dog king of Boston." (One wag has suggested that a blood test would reveal tiny hot dogs along with white and red cells in their bloodstreams.)

Terry Moore calls the restaurant business one of instant

gratification. He says he finds it very rewarding and doesn't even consider it real work.

Diane Selby of Hail Columbia began her food career shortly after high school, working at the famous Toll House in Wakefield, Massachusetts (where the cookie of the same name was first made). Later she and her husband, Donald, started a restaurant in California. They've had ups and downs with their restaurant, as just about everyone does, but as she says, "No matter how awful an experience you've had, if an opportunity comes up again, you're ready to go."

She adds, "Every night's different. You never have the same mix of people.

"It's fun," she concludes, "it's really fun."

Joe Beyer, proprietor of Pontchartrain Wine Cellar (where Cold Duck was invented) in Detroit, still feels the same zest for the restaurant business he felt when he began in the fifties. "Hell," he told me with a laugh, "this business is like being at a party every night."

How to Use This Book

You now have a small taste of the pros and cons of opening a restaurant. You will find in the following pages much information intended to help you as you plan and begin your business adventure.

In Chapter 2, "Sketching In the Outlines," you'll find a discussion of methods for thoroughly planning your dream, starting with focusing your vision.

In the four chapters that follow, the focus moves to the preliminaries to setting up a restaurant. These matters include "Determining Your Market and Scouting Your Site" (Chapter 3), "Real-Estate Options" (Chapter 4), "Creating a Business Plan" (Chapter 5), and finally, dealing with the harsh realities of "Financing, Taxes, the Law, and Insurance" (Chapter 6).

Most people starting out in the restaurant business seek out a workable space then tailor it to their needs. Thus Chapter 7, "Shaping the Space," is all about creating your premises, from laying out the kitchen and the dining room to the often tricky business of working well with architects and contractors.

Chapter 8, "Food and Drink: The Heart of the Matter," features information on the fare to be served. You will find discussions of planning, pricing, and designing menus, as well as dealing with wholesalers.

Every well-run restaurant relies on efficient systems to help the operation run smoothly. Chapter 9, "Setting Up Systems," is all about devising such strategies, from inventory control through billing, reservations, portion control, and food handling.

Unless you take over a complete and fully operational restaurant, you will probably need to equip and furnish your space. Chapter 10, "Equipping and Furnishing Your Restaurant," will help guide you through the many intricacies of choosing and buying both kitchen and dining-room equipment, from cooking surfaces and refrigeration through china, crystal, and decorative accessories.

The staff is almost as vital an element to the success of a restaurant as the food. Chapter 11, "Your Staff," features discussions on staffing needs, and hiring, training, and managing employees.

After all the work described in the previous chapters, you can create a first-class restaurant—but you still have to let the world know that you're opening your doors. The last chapter, "Getting the Word Out," discusses useful kinds of advertising, publicity and public relations, and methods for using them most efficiently.

If your restaurant works, and many do despite the failure rate, you may find that you can take time off, travel, live well, see your children, even open another restaurant. Just don't go into it thinking that it's an easy life.

You also shouldn't believe that whether you succeed is largely a matter of luck, magic, or the result of knowing the secret. There are no secrets, just as there are no new restaurant concepts waiting to be discovered. On the other hand, you give yourself every possible advantage when you plan your establishment as thoroughly as possible. The better you can think it through on paper, as well as in your head, the better your chances.

Doing it right is critical: you must manage all of the elements of your restaurant so that they work together seamlessly. Doing it right is also a matter of serving first-quality food, be it Tex-Mex or haute cuisine fresh from the kitchen, without a great deal of fuss from your staff, in a pleasant atmosphere. Doing it right means your customers leave feeling they have gotten good value by coming to your restaurant.

It is the aspiring restaurateur who wants to do it right for whom this book has been written. So take your time, think it through, plan well, and open the best restaurant you know how. Here's hoping it proves a most rewarding experience.

CHAPTER

2

Sketching In the Outlines

Before you begin seriously considering your own restaurant, you should try to determine what you want and need out of the business.

Does that sound painfully obvious? It may well be, but a surprising number of people fail to think through many decisions in advance of making them.

The time for close self-examination of your goals and desires is before you open your restaurant. You may have a concept in your mind of what the restaurant will be like—but ask yourself, "Does it suit me and my temperament?"

Do you know what role you will play? If you're an early bird or a night owl, does it suit your schedule? Will you feel comfortable in its environs, as if you belong there? Is the place a realistic reflection of your talents, character, and energies?

Many people, including both winners and losers in the restaurant game, don't have a clear goal beyond opening and being successful. Some think they have developed a concept that is surefire; others believe they have the perfect site; still others have complete confidence in their abilities to put perfect food on the table. Yet relatively few have worked through a more personal analysis and determined how they themselves fit into the picture.

As Gary Goldberg says, "It really is important to analyze your reasons for opening a restaurant." Thinking through your reasons and developing your concept may help you realize that despite all the romantic visions you may have, it's a business venture you are embarking upon. You must reach a balanced understanding: your ideals need to be both understood and integrated into a practical plan for success.

Focusing Your Vision

In successful restaurants there is something that draws customers in and makes them return. Occasionally, a lack of competition may provide a clientele. But these days, given the proliferation of restaurants, return business is usually due to something else.

In most successful restaurants there's an attitude or a personality. It's the product of someone's vision and a confident sense of how-we-do-it-here that infuses the business. The kitchen and waiting staff feel it; it gets passed on to the customer, too. That individualized specialness is as likely to be found in a flourishing fast-food franchise as it is at the finest haute cuisine restaurant.

Restaurateur George Lang says that were his son foolish enough to want to enter the business, he would advise him: "Just as a woman should wear what looks good on her and not the fashion of the day, a restaurateur should run the kind of restaurant that suits his or her talent and pocketbook."

Your talent may be for cooking, or managing, or creating an atmosphere. Your interests may lie in opening a café, coffee shop, family restaurant, bistro, or intimate gourmet restaurant. But the key is to match your interest with your talents, to seek another match with the public's needs and wishes, and then to make it happen.

"Every restaurant should have a point of view in every-thing," George Lang continues. His own restaurant, Café des Artistes, is one such place. As its proprietor describes it, "The Café is a tailored understatement, a form of reverse snobbism."

The menu, Lang says, offers "no defenseless food studded with canned truffles, no flambéed food, no designer dishes. And everything [is] called by its God-given name." Typical of the approach is the method of serving champagne. Rather than dispatching a waiter with a bottle, ice, and a stand for a big production number at your table, champagne arrives at the table in a carafe.

Yet the place has its own special chemistry: the Café des Artistes has frequently been called the most romantic restaurant in New York, a city with thousands of restaurants, hundreds of which aspire to charm and flatter every customer.

At the Old Mill in South Egremont, Massachusetts, the vision remains constant. Terry and Juliet Moore have designed a small menu, with an emphasis on all fresh food served in a comfortable atmosphere.

From the moment you walk in you feel welcomed. While you dine you never feel rushed. The service is informed but reserved, the setting a converted mill building that has a time-less character that is both elegant and casual. The repeat busi-ness the Moores have drawn to the Old Mill has made it a success.

Donald and Diane Selby knew what they wanted out of their restaurant shortly after seeing the Inn Between, a seedy bar and café that had just gone up for sale. "I think that's the first thing we designed in our heads," Mrs. Selby remembers.

They asked themselves a question. "What does this area lack?" And they answered it with their casual yet also inno-vative but simple American cuisine. But they also asked them-selves a harder question: "What could we offer that people would come to? We didn't want to be snooty-snobby, we just wanted to be quietly elegant. You could come in and relax and eat good food nicely prepared, well served, pretty to look at, and all fresh."

These people—and the success they have attained with

their restaurants—may make the process sound simple, but it isn't.

Consider this contrasting story. Paulette and Kenny Merlino knew that for their first independent venture into the food world they wanted to open a hot-dog joint. Their grandfather had started a chain of such simple hot-dog restaurants in Boston more than fifty years earlier. Called Joe and Nemo's, the hot-dog stands had become their father's business and so they grew up around it.

"Kenny's thing was to have what our father had, because there wasn't really anything like it in New York," recalls Paulette.

They felt strongly that what New York needed was to have hot dogs like those in Boston. "We had it fixed in our heads that people were going to have steamed hot dogs, whether they liked it or not. 'Steam is clean' was our motto. Somehow we didn't think it mattered that New Yorkers like grilled hot dogs."

They didn't have a source of immense capital—essentially Kenny's savings and the backing of a friend—so they knew it would have to be very simple. It was to be a hip version of what they knew so well, and it worked, being very small. They had a window to the street, a counter with four stools, and one booth.

When they moved and expanded their operation, however, they somehow lost the clarity of vision that had initially guided them. They were so busy trying to open the bar and grill that they never really sat down and talked it through. Serving well-prepared and interesting food was important to Paulette, so they hired a highly trained chef to create a more extensive menu of upscale bistro-style food to go along with their hot dogs. Yet Kenny wanted to create a neighborhood joint where people would come to watch a ball game and have a few dogs, but he didn't really want to deal with the food.

Hot Diggity Bar and Grill opened and did okay for several years. They drew some loyal neighborhood customers and their ebullient personalities kept things lively. Yet the restaurant never really found its niche: part of the explanation is that the brother-and-sister team never found a focus and, over time, their differing views became a source of irritation.

Another incomplete restaurant vision is one that my father-in-law has been mulling over for years. It would be the perfect restaurant, he says, and his planning is precise in its way.

He doesn't have all the details worked out—he's not a restaurateur and he knows it—but in his idle musing he sees a place in which the food will be good, plain cooking (meat and potatoes, always potatoes). Even more important, he says, there will never be a carrot or leaf of spinach on his menu. He thinks of it as the ideal restaurant, and so far has elicited the approval of a number of his acquaintances.

For your restaurant, however, you'll need to develop your concept more thoroughly and back it up with thorough planning. And there's nothing like experience to help you assess your preliminary notions of what it is your restaurant should be.

KNOW THY RESTAURANT

Before you open the doors—even before you invest the first dollar—you should look to your creative self for what it is you want your restaurant to be. Perhaps the following queries can stimulate a consideration of what truly are your aspirations.

- What do you notice first in a restaurant? The decor, the service staff, the food at the next table?
- What sort of restaurants do you most often eat in? What do your favorites have in common?
- Compare your favorite eating place to your least favorite: what is done differently?
- Which is more important to you: price, service, setting, or the food?

- Which is more important: food quantity, quality, or selection?
- If you've worked in restaurants, what did you find most irksome as an employee?
- As a restaurant worker, what aspect did you find most appealing about each of the places you worked?

Get Experience or Get Help

Terry Moore started as a cabin boy on the *Queen Mary* at age sixteen. Over the next seven years he moved up through the ranks to the first-class dining rooms. Upon his return to terra firma, he managed fine restaurants from San Francisco to New York.

For Terry Moore, the next step was quite logical. If you have been lucky enough to have already worked in a restaurant for some time (preferably at all the levels from dishwasher to manager), then you have already experienced the pace and some of the demands of the business. For you, too, the leap into restaurateurship may seem the obvious next move.

Many successful restaurateurs believe that the only way to learn the business is to work in it. George Lang advises no one to start a restaurant without at least thirty years' experience and that you should be about thirty years old. Such wisecracking aside, how do you go about getting experience?

The single best source of knowledge about restaurants is other restaurants. And not just the front of the house, either, where the patrons are, but the kitchen, the food storage area, the delivery entrance, the desk with the account books, and the rest. So it's a good idea, if possible, to work in a restaurant or two so you can experience the business firsthand.

Yet you don't have to spend the next ten years accumulating lessons and dreaming about your establishment. Gary Goldberg, who along with being a restaurant consultant, runs the Culinary Arts Program at the New School in New York, reports that the majority of people who come to him interested in opening restaurants have come from successful careers in other fields.

Kenny Merlino started a successful vintage clothing business before succumbing to the lure of hot dogs. Sherry Delamarter, co-owner of four popular theme restaurants in New York, has a master's in communication and worked in television and video in Louisville before opening her first restaurant.

Joe Beyer's interest in the restaurant business came early. He enrolled in restaurant management school but soon found that the lure of fraternity parties, basketball, and a million other things interfered. After he and the school came to a parting of the ways, he became a professional photographer and worked at that before taking over at Pontchartrain Wine Cellar in 1957.

Bill Ross, owner of Hickory Bill's, was a social worker in the Pittsfield, Massachusetts, schools before the barbecuing bug took full hold and he switched to catering. Now he practices his social work in the restaurant. Michele Miller began a successful bakery with a friend because they both liked to bake. After selling that, she went on to cook for a private family, start another restaurant, and then go into catering before starting the Boiler Room Café in Southfield, Massachusetts, almost as an accident.

Some aspiring restaurateurs seek professional training rather than apprenticeship. There are over five hundred schools operating around the country that prepare people to enter the restaurant field. Many of these are geared toward the working chef, but many have courses in management as well. The offerings of such schools range from university degrees in hotel and restaurant management to straightforward vocational training.

Such courses are offered through state colleges, community colleges, private colleges, and universities. Vocational and technical schools offer a wide range of programs as well. If you are interested in exploring such formal training, the National

Restaurant Association (20 North Wacker Drive, Chicago, Illinois 60606; (312) 782-1703) can provide you with a list of schools in your area. Almost every state has at least one restaurant association and these can also be valuable sources of information about educational programs.

If working in a restaurant or going to school for a semester or two doesn't fit your timetable, there is another alternative. You might consider hiring the services of a restaurant consultant to help you get started.

For many people, a restaurant consultant becomes as important an adviser as a lawyer or accountant. Sometimes they can help save your bacon in ways you could never anticipate in advance. You can use their services as much as you want and can afford.

Such people can advise you on every aspect of your proposed restaurant from conception through the opening and beyond, or they can help with specific areas, depending on your needs. For many people, consultants provide needed expertise only in certain areas, like pricing or advertising.

However you employ a consultant, an outside professional has the added advantage of being able to see and evaluate aspects of your proposed business with eyes unblinded by emotion and dreams. A restaurant consultant doesn't get caught up thinking about your aunt Trudy's kitchen, or your first visit to that German rathskeller with your parents back when you were fourteen. He or she is looking at a business venture, plain and simple, with an uncomplicated desire to make it work for you. Your success, after all, is a reflection of that consultant's skill and expertise.

For more information on finding a consultant, contact the National Restaurant Association, your state restaurant association, or ask around.

There's a lot of planning still ahead of you. As Gary Goldberg says, "People are always amazed when I tell them how many things they need to do. But if you do it before you're spending money and desperate to open, it really saves you a ton of headaches." We will address much of that planning process in the chapters that follow.

Once you have the general outlines in your mind and you've begun to develop your concept, it is time to begin thinking about the million and one other elements necessary to open your own restaurant. That is, the one restaurant that is a clear product of your own special point of view.

CHAPTER

3

Determining Your Market and Scouting Your Site

Before you put yourself on the front lines by opening your dream restaurant, it's a wise idea to do some basic research into your market.

This involves studying the businesses that are already in your area, determining how your place of business would fit in, and finding possible sites for your restaurant. By investigating the existing businesses in your area—and by identifying any unfulfilled needs—you will be able to target more easily your own efforts.

To start with, is the area you want to open your restaurant in growing? If it is, there is a good chance that more restaurants would be welcomed. If the population is essentially constant or declining, you should consider carefully whether a need really exists for the kind of establishment you are planning. Be sure, too, that the people you will be serving are ready for the pricing scales you are planning upon.

Is the population constant year round, or is there an influx of summer or winter people on vacation? If the population in your area doesn't shift with the seasons, you'll probably want to look at the restaurants that already are successful and try to learn as much as you can about what makes them successful. If your area draws vacationers, it will probably be able to handle proportionately more restaurants than an area that relies on its year-round residents. It may also be able to handle a wide variety of restaurants, from fast food to gourmet.

Is the population young or rapidly aging? If the population tends toward the younger end of the spectrum, the greater are your chances that a lot of people eat out fairly often. A more youthful crowd also tends to like more exotic and trendy foods. In areas where a large portion of the community is composed of retired people, people tend to eat their meals out, too, but the main criteria for selecting restaurants are less adventuresome: often modest prices, plain food, and early hours are key considerations.

Is there a healthy business community? Are businesses starting or moving out of your area with a worrisome frequency? If you are in an area with a healthy business community, you may find that you will want to focus on lunch or business dinners for the bulk of your business; plan accordingly. If the business community in the area is increasing, you may also find that there is a positive need for a well-located restaurant.

Are you in or near a cultural center? Such areas draw people from greater distances who then need to eat out. If there are museums nearby, focusing on the lunch trade might be a good idea in order to dovetail your business with the needs of the museum goers. If your site is near theaters and music facilities, early and late dinners planned to coordinate with performance schedules might be the ticket.

If you have a specific site in mind, visit the area at various times of the day and week. For instance, if you are considering opening a restaurant in a business area, you will need to visit your market area during the workday, in the evening, and on weekends to be able to determine patterns, the flow of traffic, and to gauge the potential clientele. An area that empties completely at night, like many urban centers, will mean that you have to rely on the breakfast or lunch trade for the bulk of your business. In contrast, a business area that also has a residential component may extend your business. An area that is primarily residential and in which most of the population works away from home may indicate that you should rely on dinner and weekends for most of your business.

If you are considering relocating to a different area or part of the country, be sure to go on a scouting trip first—don't rely on the old friend who assures you that your fried bread will make you a mint out there.

Try to plan your visit to last a minimum of several days, preferably longer. You will need to observe life in the new setting over a period of time. If possible, make several visits at different times of the year, in order to gauge the flow of business and the types of customers to expect at various times.

For instance, if the area you choose is a resort, you'll need to see firsthand how the seasons draw people, when are the slow times, and when are the busiest. Perhaps your restaurant could draw from the locals as well as the out-of-towners, but you will best find out by close observation. The extra dollars you spend on research may save you thousands later on.

Juliet and Terry Moore invested a year visiting the Berkshire hills area of western Massachusetts. They spent weekends studying the area, its people and patterns, and looking for the best location for their restaurant. Since the Berkshires is a popular vacation and resort area, they also contacted the local visitors bureau for information regarding the people who come to visit.

They tried to figure out what people would like, both the locals and seasonal visitors, without duplicating what was already there. They believed very strongly that it was as important to be a part of the local community as it was to appeal to visitors; this approach served to broaden the clientele of their restaurant, the Old Mill, and its success attests to the care and consideration they invested in advance.

Contact local radio stations and magazines. Eventually, you may well wish to advertise, so you should know what options are available (see Chapter 12). In the meantime, however, broadcast and print media can be an invaluable source of demographic information on the local population—information that can be useful not only for advertising, but for your market research. Census information, available by contacting your local government, is another good source of demographic information.

Next, look at your competition. Are there many restaurants? What kinds of food do they serve? What range of prices do they charge? Is there a common theme that many of the restaurants in your area share? Do they sell to the same group of people, or is there a wide variety of trade?

Competition can work to your advantage, particularly if you provide something that the others do not. An area known for its variety of restaurants often draws people. They tend to think, "Oh, yes, they have a lot of nice places to eat, I'm sure we'll be happy eating over there."

You may think you know the competition very well, but it still makes sense to investigate carefully and formally the existing restaurants in the proposed area, both those that you deem competition and those that you don't. In order to study other restaurants, you will have to eat in them.

Get current copies of the menus from the most successful restaurants. Note the hours each is open, the service procedures used (do they take reservations or not? are there busboys? a sommelier?), and any peculiarities of their settings (next to an exit ramp, adjacent to the ballet company, and so on). You might even make a formal listing of the key elements of each, in order to compare and contrast them with your own plans.

While there, pay attention to and take detailed notes regarding aspects you like and dislike, noting what is missing and what is already well covered. When you see things you particularly like, such as a well-designed menu, pleasing decor, or especially good dishes, record your observations. Ask for the name of the graphic designer of any menu you particularly like. Take pictures of signs, buildings, and locations that appeal to you.

This kind of research can help later when you get down to the actual pulling together of elements for your restaurant.

The National Restaurant Association publishes a guide to

restaurant incomes around the country that is broken down by location and food type. This guide provides only averages, but can be very useful in giving you general guidelines about competitive prices in particular areas.

Another method of analyzing the market is to find a model restaurant and study it. It should be your ideal restaurant, in some or all ways. It need not be in the area where you plan to open. You might introduce yourself to the owner and tell of your plans, explaining that you want to learn as much about the restaurant as possible, would he or she be willing to teach you? You might even apply for a job, with the understanding that you would like to work in as many areas of the restaurant as possible.

A favorite story of mine concerns an aspiring restaurateur who found his model restaurant in Florida. He practically haunted the place for three days, taking pictures of every possible aspect. On the third day the management grew tired of his persistence and threw him out—literally. The last few pictures he took were strangely skewed, since he snapped them while he was being picked up bodily and deposited outside.

It wasn't the best approach, perhaps, but you can be sure he learned a great deal.

Here is an example of how I might go about discovering my market.

I live in a rural area that has recently been discovered by weekenders and summer people from New York City. Outsiders are buying property and building expensive houses. In general, the newcomers are a well-off lot, perhaps not quite as wealthy as before the stock-market crash of a few years ago, but still here and accustomed to eating out often.

I've checked out the restaurants within a radius of about fifteen miles. The restaurants tend to fall within two categories: very good and fairly expensive or cheap and family style. I've noticed that the local year-round people frequent the cheap and family-style restaurants and the pizza places more than they do the fancier restaurants. The very good restaurants appear to rely on the weekenders, tourists, and other visitors looking for an evening of rustic charm.

In short, there are few restaurants offering a middle

ground, such as a companionable place with moderately priced but up-to-date food.

There are also few ethnic restaurants, and perhaps the best model is to be found in that category. In a town about twenty-five miles away there is a family-run Italian restaurant that draws both local clientele and people who are willing to drive thirty or forty miles for an authentic-tasting meal. It's not a grand restaurant, just good food and fair prices.

That's what I think would work: a good, convenient Italian restaurant to appeal to both groups of people.

THE RESTAURANT PROFILES

In thinking how you want your restaurant to look and feel, you should certainly compare your vision to as many existing restaurants as possible. Visit them, eat in them, talk to the owners, learn as much as you can.

In trying different styles on for size, you might also consider the restaurants profiled in the following pages. They represent a range of new and traditional eateries—all of which can claim critical and financial success.

Café des Artistes
1 West 67th Street
New York, NY 10023

Proprietor: George Lang, owner since 1975

Year established: 1915

Seating: 107

Price range: About $45 per person, or more for dinner (not including wine or drinks); prix fixe dinner $30

Meals served: Lunch and dinner seven days; brunch Saturday and Sunday.

Number of employees: 82

Market: A broad range of well-heeled customers, including the noteworthy from the arts and business communities.

Menu

The menu changes daily, and features hearty and eclectic food with a European bent, "the kind of food your mother would cook if she were a good cook," according to Lang. "For decades I have tried to convince restaurateurs and chefs that they don't have to bow to trends. Even though the use of guns is increasing every year, there is no known instance of a guest threatening a restaurateur at gunpoint with 'Put that dish on the menu or your life!' "

Atmosphere and Decor

Bustling, cheerful, romantic. Murals by Howard Chandler Christy of exuberantly beautiful nude demoiselles set off the beamed ceiling, green leather banquettes, gleaming crystal, and profusion of potted plants in the windows.

"While ambience is very important, unless you plan to operate the kind of restaurant which is more show business than food business, the taste and appearance of the food is still what matters," according to Lang.

Signature Dishes

Salmon Four Ways (appetizer): slices of dill-marinated gravlax, smoked salmon, poached salmon, and a small mound of salmon tartar; braised beef with gingersnap gravy.

Hiring Philosophy

"Surround yourself with extraordinarily talented people who share your philosophies and are pleasant to be around so you don't waste time with emotional upheavals."

Remarks

When Lang bought the café in 1975, it was in decline. He had the faded murals restored to their former glory, just as he set about restoring the restaurant's reputation.

He believes that one should "control as many areas of one's restaurant as possible," and that "every restaurant should have a point of view in everything." To this end he has created a place where people come to eat perfectly prepared nontrendy food, well served, in a charming atmosphere.

Lang calls the café a "tailored understatement," a suitable summary that characterizes both the droll Mr. Lang and his wonderful landmark restaurant.

Pontchartrain Wine Cellar
234 West Larned Street
Detroit, MI 48226

Proprietor: Joe Beyer, owner since 1971

Year established: 1935

Seating: 86 in the main dining room plus a private dining room seating 40

Price range: Complete dinners range from $15.95 to $19.95; lunch entrées range from $5.95 to $7.50

Meals served: Lunch and dinner Monday through Friday; dinner only Saturday; closed Sunday; closed the first two weeks of July.

Number of employees: About 30

Market: The lunch business is clublike, drawing from attorneys, bankers, artists. Dinner brings people from the suburbs who come into the city for dinner and cultural events.

Menu

The continental bistro-style menu is comfortingly classic, though sprinkled with occasional new items. Trendy food is not the point here, but well-prepared satisfying food has made the restaurant an institution. "We serve the best snails in town," says Joe Beyer. Wine (over a hundred different ones) and beer are served, but no hard liquor.

Atmosphere and Decor

Dark paneling, brick walls, and dark red banquettes help establish the tone. "It's romantic," says Beyer. "A lot of people come to celebrate events such as anniversaries."

The dinner atmosphere is warm and welcoming with tablecloths, fresh flowers, and candlelight; at lunch, the clublike, comfortable quality is enhanced by tables set more simply with place mats.

Signature Dishes

Appetizer: escargots. Entrées: lake perch lightly breaded and seasoned with garlic, deep-fried; pickerel rolled in potato breading, broiled and served on a bed of applesauce flavored with lingonberries; rosettes of lamb. Dessert: cheesecake. The restaurant still mixes its 1937 invention, Cold Duck (two parts champagne to one part Burgundy).

Hiring Philosophy

"We make it an easy place to work, nobody's beating someone on the back," says Joe Beyer. "I'm on the floor a lot. Everyone sees that it's not beneath me to clear a table, clean it, and set it." Beyer has one waiter who has been with him for twenty-five years and a waitress who goes back to the fifties. When they need to hire a staff member, the word is put out through the staff, who invariably recommend someone.

Remarks

"We're not out to impress people. We try to be honest and straightforward in our approach and make people feel comfortable. Our people are pleasant and always gracious to customers. Many of our customers are regulars, and when you can call them by name, it makes a difference.

"I've always felt that you could go out and if the decor is cold and uncomfortable, it takes away from the food, or that if you encounter jerks, it damages the experience. We try to make people feel at ease."

Cowgirl Hall of Fame
519 Hudson Street
New York, NY 10014

Proprietors: Sherry Delamarter and Joel Gordin.

Year established: 1989

Seating: 70

Price range: Entrées $8 to $15

Meals served: Lunch and dinner; beer, wine, and cocktails available.

Number of employees: About 15

Market: A mixture of young and not so young, conservative and hip.

Menu
Texas home-style food and barbecue with a few vegetarian dishes as a concession to New Yorkers.

Signature Dishes
Chicken-fried steak with cream gravy and biscuits; barbecued beef brisket and pork spareribs; Frito pie.

Atmosphere and Decor
Associated with the Cowgirl Hall of Fame in Hereford, Texas, the restaurant honors a different member of the Hall of Fame three times a year by displaying related memorabilia such as trophies and awards, a fact sheet about the

honoree, and serving favorite dishes or specialties of her home state.

The decor in general is casual, with vintage rodeo posters lining the walls along with other western kitsch, including a stuffed armadillo and an extensive barbed-wire display.

Business Philosophy

The five partners in Delamarter's four restaurants act as a collective. The owners for the most part have worked in the restaurants, building "sweat equity" and earning the right to own stock.

"Everybody likes to have a restaurant and say, 'That's my restaurant. Go over—they'll take care of you,'" says Delamarter. "They don't want to be there seven days a week and deal with dirty rags, or a short order, or a kitchen that can't speak English. . . . They aren't there for the customer."

Remarks

On the importance of advertising: Sherry Delamarter believes in only the simplest of advertising: "We buy our customers drinks," she says.

When Delamarter and her partners opened their first restaurant, Tortilla Flats, they made just about every possible mistake, from a bad location to no business strategy. And yet, three restaurants later, they seem to thrive.

Perhaps it's due to the solid concepts they develop. Tortilla Flats provided good, fresh, cheap Mexican food, when no one else in town did. Gulf Coast, their Cajun and Creole restaurant, brought the then strictly regional cuisine to the Big Apple. Sugar Reef, their Caribbean outlet, followed shortly thereafter, and was soon copied by hordes of imitators.

Cowgirl Hall of Fame is perhaps closest to Texas-born Delamarter's heart, as she tours the place in cowgirl outfit, complete with tiny cowboy-boot earrings.

The Old Mill
South Egremont, MA 01258

Proprietors: Juliet and Terry Moore.

Year established: 1978

Seating: About 65 in the dining room.

Price range: Entrées $14 to $22

Meals served: Dinner, seven nights June to October; closed Mondays balance of year; beer, wine, and liquor available.

Number of employees: 15

Market: Local people out for a special evening, vacationers who come to the Berkshires for skiing and scenery, and weekenders from New York.

Menu

High-quality, simply prepared fresh food, featuring fish. "We've never made any real demands on sauces or tried to gussy up [the food] in any way," says Terry Moore.

Signature Dishes

Herbed goat cheese served with breads; sautéed shrimp with artichokes, tomato, garlic, and parsley; crème brûlée.

Atmosphere and Decor

Originally a grist mill and then an antiques shop before being converted to a restaurant in 1978, the Old Mill blends well with the surrounding picturesque village. The atmosphere is welcoming and understated.

White walls and linen set off the dark ceiling beams, stenciled wide plank floors, the collection of wall-mounted antique chopping tools, and English majolica. Two tall English pine settles anchor the two ends of the dining room, and a small fireplace sets off the L-portion of the room while drawing the whole together. The setting is comfortable and purposeful.

Business Philosophy

"We offer a limited menu of fresh food, with reasonable prices in an atmosphere that is comfortable. We don't make any pretensions about dress. We're not here to win any awards with our cuisine. We train the employees never to pressure anybody to hurry or rush the service. We're here for you to come in for the next two hours and to have a wonderful time."

Remarks

The Old Mill is popular with local residents as well as vacationers and weekenders. Moore feels that being a part of the community is imperative to the success of his restaurant. He also welcomes as much competition as possible.

"I love going to restaurants around here and I like to be surrounded by good restaurants. People say, 'Aren't you worried about a restaurant opening down the road that's great? *No way!*

"If people have a great experience here and I can recommend a great experience down the road, and another great experience, people are going to leave this area and say, 'You've got to go to the Berkshires.' It just helps the area grow."

Hickory Bill's
478 West Housatonic Street
Pittsfield, MA 01201

Proprietors: William C. Ross, Kerry L. C. Ross.

Year established: 1988

Seating: 30

Price range: Dinner under $10; lunch about $5

Meals served: Lunch and dinner, six days a week.

Number of employees: 3 during the summer, 2 during the winter, varying numbers of part-time workers during the summer for catering events.

Market: People from nearby towns, vacationers, and summer visitors who are looking for something a little out of the ordinary.

Menu: Barbecue with simple accompaniments.

Atmosphere and Decor

Hickory Bill's started out in a simple dining car located next to a shopping center on the outskirts of Pittsfield. The atmosphere is very friendly. A counter at the front of the restaurant, where orders are placed, seats six. A small dining room in back and another small room provide additional seating. Patrons can pick up food for takeout, or sit down and relax with a newspaper and conversation. The decor is plain, as befits a good barbecue joint, and the company welcoming.

Signature Dishes

Pork spareribs are the hottest sellers here, closely followed by slow-cooked brisket. Chopped pork sandwiches, barbecued chicken, and barbecued beef ribs are popular as well. Mexican corn bread heads the list of side dishes, closely followed by collard greens and barbecued baked beans. "Everything here is a very solid item," says Bill Ross.

Remarks

In three years of operation, Hickory Bill's has outgrown its modest space and will soon be moving to a larger and more convenient location. Testaments to the quality of the food comes from the loyal patrons, most of whom drive at least thirty minutes to reach it.

Bill opened the restaurant as an outgrowth of his catering business, which still thrives. After perfecting his technique, he approached a fine restaurant in nearby Lenox, Massachusetts. When told that they never used anything not prepared in house, he philosophically returned home, having left three racks of ribs for testing. Bobbie Crosby, the owner, liked the product so much that she called up Bill's home, spoke with his daughter, and ordered twenty-five pounds—all before he reached the driveway.

Hail Columbia
1 Kinderhook Street
Chatham, NY 12037

Proprietors: Diane and Donald Selby.

Year established: 1988

Seating: 76 in two dining rooms, one an enclosed porch, the other a snug bar.

Price range: Entrées from $15 to $22

Meals served: Lunch and dinner six days a week; beer, wine, and cocktails available. After-theater supper served during the summer.

Number of employees: 16 to 18

Market: Many people from the Albany area (New York's capital, 30 miles away) who want to take a pleasant drive; weekenders, vacationers, and people attending the local summer-stock theater.

Menu
"Good food, nicely prepared, well served, pretty to look at, and all fresh," is how Diane Selby refers to the fare. Grilled pizzas and elegant pastas share the menu with bouillabaisse, duckling, and fish such as mahimahi, salmon, fresh tuna, and blue marlin.

Signature Dishes

Roasted rack of lamb encrusted in hazelnuts; escargots in red russet potatoes with garlic butter; grilled pizza with chicken, leeks, and bourbon barbecue sauce.

Atmosphere and Decor

At first glance the decor of Hail Columbia seems very Victorian. Deep red walls and banquettes mingle with antique gilt frames and rich wood tones. A converted gaslight chandelier is a focal point of the entrance area. Hunting prints line the walls. The effect, however, is not that of a studied period piece but of comfortable ease and elegance. The atmosphere is friendly, unhurried, but efficient.

Remarks

The Selbys find that being able to welcome customers with a little extra attention makes people feel good. This is particularly helpful since many of their clients make a special trip from the Albany area.

"If you have a small enough restaurant, it makes a great deal of difference if you can call the majority of people by name. If you can welcome enough of the repeaters by name, they become loyal," says Diane.

The Selbys also offer wisdom for people about to renovate a space. Diane advises that you find a contractor you know. "One that's done work for you and that you like and you trust. And then, you should never trust them. Never go on time and materials. Make sure you get bids. Those are my final words on that."

In the long run their space turned out beautifully for them, but not without great added expense and heartache.

The Boiler Room Café
Norfolk Southfield Road
Southfield, MA 01259

Proprietor: Michele Miller.

Year established: 1987

Seating: 36

Price range: Entrées $13 to $20

Meals served: During the summer, lunch and dinner Thursday through Monday; during the winter, dinner Thursday through Monday, lunch on weekends.

Numbers of Employees: 6 or 7 during the heat of the summer.

Market: People looking for something a little special, drawn mainly from second-home owners in the area and a hard core of locals who come every weekend.

Menu

"Full-flavored and well conceived," according to Moira Hodgson reviewing in *The New York Times*; "unpretentious and hearty," according to Michele Miller.

"We're one of the only places in the area that makes real risotto," says Miller. Miller is also known for her baked goods, since she ran a bakery in nearby Lenox for several years.

Signature Dishes

Risotto, cioppino, homemade baguette, homemade sausage, Virginia baby back ribs, wild mushroom lasagna.

Atmosphere and Decor

The restaurant is housed in an actual boiler room to which Miller did as little as possible. The atmosphere is cozy and intimate, but a little sophisticated despite the mismatched chairs and imperfect paint. She has hung good art on the walls. Jazz piano music on the weekends entertains and soothes.

Remarks

The restaurant started almost by accident. "I didn't know anything about anything when I started," says Michele Miller. She and a friend started a bakery in Lenox, Massachusetts, which they ran for several years. After selling it—"I was pooped," she says—she took a couple of years off and then started the Inn on the Green in New Marlborough, Massachusetts, with a couple she knew. After two years or so, she went on her own to cater. The catering business flourished and before long she found that she needed more space.

She found the boiler room, and before long one thing led to another. The owner of the building wanted to serve lunch, so they served it. Soon they had a restaurant with sixteen seats, and before they knew it they opened another room to accommodate an additional twenty.

When asked her feelings about the business, she says, "I love it, but I don't know if I'd do it again, it's constant."

Given her record, however, I'd be prepared to say she would.

DC3
2800 Donald Douglas Loop North
at the Santa Monica Airport
Santa Monica, CA 90405

Proprietors: Bruce Marder, David Price, August Spier, William Hufferd.

Year established: 1989

Seating: 200

Meals served: Lunch Tuesday through Friday; dinner seven nights; Sunday brunch.

Number of employees: About 60

Market: Business people at lunch; denizens of the Los Angeles area and travelers from all over the world.

Menu

Grilled and braised meats and fish with worldwide influences including the Pacific rim, Italy, France, and Greece. French- and American-style desserts.

Signature Dishes

Chicken "pancake" with grapefruit, serrano chilies and grapefruit-butter sauce; rack of lamb with herbes de Provence; braised veal shank with Madeira-and-thyme sauce; orange soufflé.

Atmosphere and Decor

Owner Bruce Marder hired artist Charles Arnoldi to create a warm and personal restaurant out of an almost runway-size area. He created a restaurant reminiscent of a floating space station. It is filled with sculptural forms, marbled and granite surfaces, and interesting textures. "Entering the restaurant is a little like preparing for a rocket launch," wrote Caroline Bates in *Gourmet*.

Remarks

Most people don't think of going to the airport for a first-rate meal. Nor does one usually associate good food with a restaurant in which so much emphasis has been put on the design and decor. But DC3 is different on all counts.

Caroline Bates calls the food nothing less than terrific. Owner Bruce Marder is also a master at determining California trends. Says Bates: "He is a prescient restaurateur who understands what Angelenos want to eat and drink even before they know it themselves."

Location

According to a tried-and-true rule of real estate, there are three key determinants of property values: location, location, and location. The same rule might well be applied to successful restaurants, probably more than to any other kind of business.

Finding a site with the right location is one of the most important things you can do. If you situate your restaurant off the proverbial beaten path, you may have to work doubly hard to get the word out and to convince people to travel out of their way to cross your threshold.

This is not to say that restaurants with seemingly poor locations don't become phenomenally successful, or that others with perfect-seeming locations never go bust in a matter of months. Neither is true.

Many restaurants succeed wildly despite an unfortunate location. Sherry Delamarter could hardly have picked a less auspicious location when she opened Tortilla Flats, the first of her four successful restaurants in New York. Tortilla Flats opened near the banks of the Hudson River in a desolate part of town. It was inconvenient to public transportation, far from any thriving neighborhoods, and on a street and block heavily frequented by prostitutes.

The ladies of the night did oblige Sherry and her partners by moving down a few blocks when the restaurateurs explained that they were trying to start a family restaurant. Perhaps that surprising cooperative spirit was an omen, since despite its inaccessibility, the restaurant succeeded. Good word of mouth, terrific reviews, a real need for the good food they served, and the personality of the owners overcame the disadvantage of a miserable location.

At Hickory Bill's, situated on the edge of Pittsfield, Massachusetts, townspeople find the location out of the mainstream. Yet people from towns half an hour away think nothing of the distance.

The Boiler Room Café in Southfield, Massachusetts, is out of the flow of traffic, which led to a slow start. But this also contributed to a loyal, local clientele, many of whom work in the tourist industry and like to escape it when they eat out themselves. A couple of favorable reviews served to make people seek out the restaurant, doubling the business in one summer.

Brian McNally is another immensely successful restaurateur in New York. His restaurants usually become the hot spots in town for the trendiest of the trendy; yet he has a very simple business formula. He consciously selects undesirable locations with dirt-cheap rents. When the word gets around that Brian McNally is about to open another restaurant, people take notice. When they open, no matter how deserted the neighborhood is or how hard it is to find (that's the taxi driver's job in New York, anyway), McNally's restaurants always seem to have a line at the door.

Most people, however, can't take the chance on a bad location. Look hard and, if necessary, look long to find the spot that augurs best for your particular restaurant.

Spotting the Right Site

Once you have identified the general vicinity you would like to be in, it's time to play Find the Right Site.

You'll want to look carefully at the neighborhood you've selected. There might be a perfect space just waiting for you to come by and claim, but more likely you'll need to use some imagination. In all likelihood, that means plain, old-fashioned legwork.

Legwork, while exhausting, can be one of the best methods for locating a site. You choose an area and walk or drive around it, studying businesses and generally conducting an informal market survey. Only by seeing an area and the people who frequent it do you get a real sense of what's available. You may not ever have noticed a particular building that when, examined carefully, emerges as suiting your needs exactly.

You may also find that you don't have a definite idea of which neighborhood you want to be in and that you need help narrowing the range. You can contact real-estate companies who are in the business of providing commercial spaces. They can often help narrow the choices and the areas in which to look.

The word-of-mouth approach is not to be underestimated

either. You might want to pass the news of your interest to a few well-chosen friends and relatives. Often the word gets out and comes back to you about possibilities without the expense of an agency commission between you and the seller or lessor.

Don't overlook the advertisements in the real-estate sections of newspapers and local magazines.

You will probably want to employ all of these methods—unless, of course, you happen to strike it lucky and find the perfect spot right away.

Keep in mind that different kinds of restaurants are best suited to certain kinds of locations. Carryout restaurants and breakfast-and-lunch counters or diners often are best located in visible, high-traffic areas where people are likely to stop on their way to or from work. Often the neighboring businesses are retailers or service businesses like cleaners. Franchise restaurants are often best located along well-traveled routes with easy access from the road and plenty of parking, or in shopping malls or enclosed shopping areas with lots of foot traffic. In such sites, seating (and overhead expenses) may be shared with other franchise operations.

Family dinner restaurants are often located near well-traveled routes not far from residential areas, and with plenty of parking.

Restaurant bars or bistros can often attract a frequent and loyal clientele when located in a residential or business neighborhood (depending on whether lunch or dinner is emphasized). If located away from such a logical setting, they need to be easily found and to provide plenty of parking.

Gourmet restaurants can be located in a variety of places, since people tend to seek them out, and prosperity is likely to be due in large part to word-of-mouth advertising, publicity, and newspaper reviews. They often do well in out-of-the-way places, provided that they are fairly easy to reach and near enough to some draw—it might be a cultural center, or area of natural beauty—that people find it convenient to break their usual patterns.

Considering the Space

Unless you have a lot of money, you will probably want to look for a building that either is already a restaurant, or one that could be made into one easily on a reasonable budget. If you find a site that appeals to you particularly but that is already operating as a restaurant, it won't hurt to inquire if the owner is willing to sell.

In general, it's best to find an existing restaurant space rather than try to build or convert one. This is especially true if your budget is tight. These days, approximately *half* the expense of building a restaurant consists of mechanical costs. These include heating, ventilation, and air-conditioning systems (HVAC); water, gas, and electrical lines; fire stairs; kitchen equipment; and a thousand other details.

To determine if a building could feasibly be turned into a restaurant, you'll need to do some homework. Every town has laws and regulations regarding restaurants. Contact the appropriate local authorities or chamber of commerce for information regarding zoning, building laws, health-department requirements, environmental regulations, and local taxes.

A commercial real-estate agent may be aware of some of the local regulations and requirements and thus be able to save you a certain amount of homework, particularly when it comes to spaces that would be inappropriate for a restaurant. You must be aware, however, that real-estate agents owe their first allegiance to those who pay them—namely the lessor or seller, not you.

Local planning officials and the chamber of commerce can be useful in determining the growth of a particular area. You may hear rumors that a big office complex is about to be built, or is built, rented, and the hottest thing to hit town in two decades. Conversely, you may learn that the handsome building is nearly empty and its owners on the verge of bankruptcy.

By checking with local planning officials you may get a more accurate idea of actual timetables and possible uncertainties regarding the area's growth. Once again, real-estate agents and chamber-of-commerce representatives exist to serve certain interests; in some instances, they may not be yours and you'll need to be able to separate exaggerated and rosy possibilities from likely realities.

LOCAL REGULATIONS

While at the planning department, you will also want to get copies of any regulations, zoning laws, and ordinances. Local officials might be able to provide other useful information about activities in the area and community groups as well.

At the very least, the office should be able to provide (or steer you toward) the following information:

1. Zoning laws that might affect where you can open a restaurant.
2. Copies of health regulations, Occupational and Safety Health Act (OSHA) standards, and other rules of which you may not be aware.
3. Parking requirements in the vicinity.
4. Outline of procedure for obtaining a conditional use permit and/or zoning variance, if needed.
5. A copy of the current regional planning document.
6. Regulations regarding signs, both on- and off-site.
7. Names of the planning director and each of the planning board members.
8. The names of all local officials, including mayor, council members, or supervisors, who serve the district.
9. The existence and name of any nonofficial advisory planning committee and how to get in touch with its president.

10. The names of any local community interest or advo-
cacy groups that might be concerned with your
business.

Keep in mind, too, that whenever you go to talk to anyone
regarding your proposed business, you're talking to potential
customers. Just by being presentable, friendly, and organized,
you serve as a walking advertisement for your nascent
business.

Where you locate your restaurant must also depend on
what you can afford. You may find the perfect site on day one
of your search: it may have everything you want from charm
to plenty of street traffic, easy access to public transportation,
ample parking, and a visible site at the heart of an area that
bustles night and day. But if you can't possibly afford the rent,
you're idling away your time thinking twice about that spot.

Even if you find a great space at a price you can afford,
however, you may run into other problems. Kenny Merlino had
a space all scoped out for his first hot-dog joint, Hot Diggity.
It was a small building in New York's Greenwich Village that
had been designed in the twenties as a gas station. It was
located in a busy part of town for foot traffic—it even had a
little parking—and best of all, it was vacant. Kenny began
negotiating with the owner, a hippie holdover from the sixties
who sold vegetables in Brooklyn.

Everything looked great. Kenny and his sister, Paulette,
could afford the rent the landlord was asking, the space was
exactly where they wanted it, and the owner seemed willing
to rent it to them. They were pretty close to closing the deal
when it became apparent that the owner of the building—who
was a vegetarian—insisted on playing an active role in the
restaurant's operation and required that they sell fruits and
vegetables and maybe sushi, in addition to hot dogs. That didn't
fit with Kenny and Paulette's concept of a hot-dog joint. So

negotiations came to an end and they found themselves pounding the pavements anew looking for another location.

Eventually, they found a tiny store in an area with a lot of foot traffic that had one particularly attractive feature. A front window opened to the street so that people could walk up and order a hot dog to go. The neighborhood wasn't quite as good as their first choice, but it served their needs and their budget.

Be patient: legwork and a little time will likely deliver you to the door of your new place of business.

And don't make the mistake one deli owner of my acquaintance did. He and his wife bought an existing business outside Chicago. The husband recalls: "It worried us at first that the place wasn't that close to home. But we said to ourselves, 'It's only about an hour from home.'

"So we ran the place for a while. Business was okay but there was one problem: even a short day of, say, eight hours, was automatically ten with the drive. Or eleven if we got stuck in traffic. And there was no way we could go home to let in, say, the meter reader.

"So we finally sold the place and bought another closer to home. It's bad enough to feel like you live at your restaurant. But then to spend more time in the car, that was too much."

So find the site you want: it may take perseverance, patience, and the intercession of Lady Luck, but the selection of where you set up shop is among the most important decisions you will make.

---

15 ELEMENTS TO CONSIDER

Regarding Location:

1. *The Area.* Do the areas you are considering fit in with your concept for the restaurant?
2. *Access.* How difficult is it to reach the restaurant,

both by car and on foot? If it is difficult to see or get to, you may have trouble attracting customers.

3. *Competition.* Are there four restaurants already on the block? What makes them different from yours? Is yours likely to be the only one for miles around?

4. *Local regulations.* What are the zoning regulations regarding restaurants? How high are the taxes in the area? If the area is growing quickly, you may face restrictive zoning and rapidly increasing taxes.

5. *Municipal and state laws.* What are the local and state laws pertaining to restaurants in your chosen area? Such laws usually stipulate health requirements, liquor service, and environmental concerns. Are they the same in neighboring towns?

6. *Population growth.* Is the area growing, is it constant, or is it seasonal? This may or may not affect your business, given the nature of your particular restaurant.

7. *Local prosperity.* An area with a certain amount of wealth is more likely able to support restaurants in a variety of price ranges, while a depressed or stagnant area may be able to support only inexpensively priced establishments.

8. *The total universe.* Where do you expect to draw your customers from? Do you expect your trade to be primarily neighborhood, local, or to travel from a distance?

9. *Demographic makeup.* Is your chosen area heavily ethnic? This may affect the type of restaurant you choose to open.

10. *Local traffic.* How much flows by the door, and of what nature? Do cars have access to parking? Is the site located on a highway on which most people whiz by at seventy?

11. *The employment pool.* In some areas there are plenty of people wanting to work in the restaurant business; in others it is a problem. For instance, in some fast-food franchises in well-to-do suburbs across the country, workers have to be transported from nearby cities because the local labor pools for minimum-wage labor have shrunk drastically.

12. *Municipal services.* Are police and fire protection

provided? Is the site connected to municipal water and sewage or will you rely on a well and septic system? What about garbage pickup? Is it provided by the city or will you need to contract separately for it? Is a service available locally? How expensive is it?

13. *Proximity to markets and suppliers.* How close is the site to wholesale markets? Will suppliers readily deliver to the area?

14. *Building capacity.* Does the building provide the amount of seating you envision for your restaurant? Is it possible to expand the site in the future, either by building or taking over a next-door building? Are variances possible if you need to expand?

15. *The lease.* What kind of lease is being offered? What are you liable for? Is there a demolition clause?

CHAPTER

4

Real-Estate Options

While you're looking for the ideal location for your restaurant, it helps to be aware of various real-estate options. At its simplest, the question is to buy or not to buy.

There are advantages and disadvantages to both options. The main advantage to a lease arrangement is that you don't have to make the large investment required for buying. On the other hand, the principal advantages of buying property are that you build equity as an investment and you control the property absolutely.

Let's look at the options individually.

Leasing the Space

When leasing (renting) a space, you are granted the right to use the building (or a designated portion thereof) for a specified amount of time.

You may encounter two basic kinds of lease: flat and percentage. Under a flat lease, you pay a fixed sum for the term. At the end of the term you are subject to an increase in the rent. A percentage lease usually requires payment of a fixed sum plus a percentage of gross sales.

All aspects of the arrangement, such as how the building is used, responsibilities for care and maintenance, and even renovation are subject to a lease agreement. This document must be in writing, for your protection, and should be vetted by your attorney.

For many people, leasing a space is the only way they can enter the business. Sometimes it's not merely a matter of having enough money to buy a building or a business, but of whether you can find one you want for sale. In many cities, restaurants take up a small portion of a huge building, so that buying space in a large building is simply not an option. In some cities the cost of real estate is so high that to buy even a small building would be prohibitively expensive except for a multimillionaire.

Leasing also avoids the long-term commitment of assuming a mortgage for the purchase of a property. If you want to get out of the business after a few years, you may find it easier to sell the unused portion of your lease, or simply to leave when the lease expires.

If you lease a property, you know how much you will be paying each month during the lease's term. This can be helpful when projecting operating expenses. You are not responsible for taxes, fluctuating mortgage rates, and certain insurance premiums. In addition, your landlord may be responsible for some of the services and maintenance of the building.

There are also compromise situations. You may actually buy and lease at the same time. For instance, you may lease a lot, but build on the site. Such situations often involve long-term leases lasting decades (ninety-nine-year leases are commonplace in some cities). If, at some point, you are unable to buy the land and need to move, you may be able to pick up— lock, stock, and restaurant—and move your business to another setting.

Leasing has its share of disadvantages as well. The most

obvious is that when the lease term expires you have contributed to the owner's equity but have built none of your own. You have no value to show for the substantial real-estate expenses you've put out.

When the current term expires, your rent could also be raised beyond your means. Your landlord may decide to cash in on you if the area of town becomes particularly desirable or if your business obviously thrives. Many owners also extract a percentage of your profits as part of the lease agreement. This, of course, limits your profitability.

You may have a great landlord who takes pains to keep the building in good shape, and then again you may not. You may find that the long-promised roof repair takes months, embarrassing you and perhaps even compromising business. If you find yourself talked into leasing equipment or furnishings already in the place, you may end up stuck with substandard goods.

Relationships can change, too. You may enter into the lease agreement with a good working relationship with your landlord. However, you cannot assume that the landlord you start with will be with you forever. Buildings, particularly in large cities, change hands with great frequency. I've heard more than a few stories about two and even three landlord changes in the course of a year or two.

At this point you're not likely to be thinking about selling your business, but several years down the road you might want out. If you lease your building, you may find it harder to sell the business, since any buyer will be bound by the terms of your rental agreement. For instance, it may contain clauses related to the type of establishment that can be run.

In most instances, the lessee is responsible for the cost of renovations or construction within the space. However, once the lease runs out and you opt to leave, you have no way to recoup that investment.

If you decide to lease, you should be sure to have an experienced attorney draw up a lease agreement. Many cities recognize a standard lease agreement that covers certain areas protected by the city. However, beyond that, your lease can be infinitely varied. Let us hope you find a landlord that you feel you can trust and with whom you develop a good relationship. That, however, should never preclude your having a properly drawn lease agreement in which all provisions are well defined in writing, agreed to by both parties. You can never tell what your relationship might be several years (or even months) down the road, or whether you will even have the same landlord.

PROPERTY CONSIDERATIONS

When considering leasing or buying a property, you should have a series of questions in your mind (or better yet, on paper) to help you decide whether to take the property or at least keep you aware of possible shortcomings.

If you know in advance, for example, that the building you want requires new wiring, you will need to add another line item to your start-up cost calculations; you might also be able to use that knowledge as a negotiating point with the owner.

Whether leasing or buying, consider these issues:

- Condition of the building, structural and cosmetic. It should meet current local codes for wiring (including 220-volt power availability), water, gas, and sewage service.
- Permitted uses for the zoning category. Are there any variances existing, or conditional uses allowed only by permit in that part of town?
- Fire rating for insurance.
- Availability of service for garbage and trash removal, snow removal, landscape maintenance.
- Off-street parking space.

For leasing in particular you should ask about:

- Long-term availability of the lease.
- Past restrictions on the licenses of tenants.
- Who is responsible for the building's insurance and what kinds are needed.
- Who is responsible for maintenance and repairs.
- Lease restrictions covering the use of the building or adjacent businesses.

Certain of these issues may well be covered in the lease agreement, as mentioned below, but the more you know ahead of time, the better a decision you can make.

And don't forget: Get It in Writing.

Lease Agreement

When setting up the agreement, ask questions about anything you don't understand. Now is the time to make everything clear. Be firm but reasonable about items you want covered in the agreement.

You may have to compromise in some areas, but be wary of a landlord who seems unreasonable on important issues. The goal is a contract that is satisfactory to both parties.

Items to be covered in the lease include:

1. Exact description of the property to be leased.
2. The monthly rent, including any possible increases and how they would be handled.
3. Term of the lease. The most desirable arrangement is a long lease with a fixed rental. Try to get options to renew with specified rent escalators if a long lease is unavailable so that you don't find yourself faced with a quadrupled rent at the end of your lease.
4. Termination notice. You will want to know the amount

of time before the lease expires before you or the landlord has to notify the other of the intent to renew.

5. Any utilities and services to be included such as heat, electricity, water, maintenance (including, if possible, a schedule), garbage pickup (again, with schedule).

6. Any equipment or furnishings to be included and any information relating to their condition or schedule for future replacement.

7. Responsibility for leasehold improvements.

8. Local laws. Does the space already conform to local laws? If the nature of the building's use changes, will the landlord take responsibility in the future for conforming with local ordinances? Will the landlord support you in petitioning for a zoning variance, should you need one?

9. Who is liable for the building? Will the owner be responsible for carrying proper insurance on the building? Most likely, you will be required to carry insurance on the business, but other insurance (fire and liability, for example) might well be the landlord's expense.

10. Sublet rights. If your business does not thrive as expected, you will want the right to lease the business to someone else to recoup at least some of your investment.

11. Lease requirements in case of force majeure or catastrophe. If a hurricane blows up or a fire destroys the building, are you released from the terms of the lease?

Buying the Space

If you can afford to buy a space, you may well find that this is the best option for a long-term commitment. As mentioned earlier, perhaps the biggest advantage is that you build equity in the property rather than paying someone else's mortgage. As the mortgage is paid down, your increasing equity can also be translated into collateral for additional cash. Remember, too, that the longer you hold on to the property, the more likely it is to increase in value, whether it contains a successful restaurant or not.

If you own the property, you have more control over its use than if you rent. The specifications for the restaurant are usually subject to zoning and other local regulations and laws, but within those parameters, you retain full control. You can set the time schedule and choose the crews and suppliers for renovating, maintenance, and construction.

As an owner, you never have to worry about your rent being increased so much that you cannot afford the space. You're not subject to the whim of a landlord and his refusal to renew a lease or a demand for a portion of your receipts.

If you ever need to leave the space, you can lease or sell it, thus making back some of your investment. You can also lease or sell the equipment separately.

There are also disadvantages to buying, of course. The most obvious is that it costs a great deal of money up front. Money is often tight when you are first starting out, and finding funding for such a large expense can be very difficult.

Another disadvantage is the long-term commitment buying implies. If you discover to your dismay that you've chosen a bad location, you can't just pick up and go: you have capital tied up in the building. If you suddenly need to leave quickly, it may be difficult to find a leaser or buyer on short notice. The large cash outlay needed to buy the property can make it difficult to find a buyer, so if you find yourself in a position of needing to get out, it may be best to find a tenant whose rent can cover the operating costs of the property.

As an owner, you are also responsible for repairs and renovations. Tax increases and insurance costs on the building are also yours to pay.

Once the closing has been completed and you own title to a building, you will begin paying for it immediately—even if the business won't be ready to open for months. This, however, is often true with leases, too.

All in all, if you can afford to buy a property and are willing to take on the responsibility of ownership, you will stand to gain more in the long run, particularly if the restaurant is successful.

When considering buying a restaurant space, you will

want to know the answers to a lot of questions that will affect your business. In addition to all the requirements for leasing (see above), you will also want to know:

- The assessed value of the land and improvements.
- Annual taxes on the property. When are they due?
- Are any restrictions on the deed, and if so, what kind?
- The presence of existing loans. If so, whether you can assume the loan, and at what interest rate.
- If there are any outstanding liens on the property.
- The structural condition of the building and property. You may want to hire an engineer to make an assessment. Don't take the word of the owner or real-estate agent.
- If there are any conditional use permits. If so, are they renewable when the property changes hands?
- Are fixtures and equipment included with the building? At what cost? What condition are they in?

Your real-estate agent may be able to answer a number of these questions. If not, contact the owner or property manager.

Leasing an Existing Restaurant

Many people start out by leasing an existing restaurant from its owner. In such an instance, you may find yourself both leasing the business and subletting the building.

Leasing a business has some of the same advantages as leasing a building. The initial investment of capital is generally much less than starting from scratch. In addition, your start-up is much quicker.

Indeed, it may be that you find yourself in a turnkey operation. The dining room, kitchen, equipment, and furnishings are all in place. Perhaps the staff is, too. You also can review the success of the restaurant by examining the sales figures and expenses. You may want to make some changes, and need capital to do so. But it is often much easier to finance an existing business for which hard numbers regarding income and expenses are available than to begin anew.

Leasing an existing restaurant has its disadvantages as well. First, why does the owner want out? The most common reason given is probably that the owner wants a change, or wants to retire. Be careful. Check things out by doing some research. Ask other businesses, observe the restaurant during slow and busy times, at all times of the week. Eat in the competition—in short, do the same sort of analysis you would do for a market study of an unopened restaurant (see page 23).

By taking over a running restaurant, you may find yourself fighting an uphill battle—trying to turn around a failing business or struggling to change the image of a tired one. You may want to consider remodeling, a change of menu, even a name change to distinguish what was there from what you are creating. If you do all this, however, you may need to rebuild your clientele as well. The old regulars who liked the place just fine before may not be happy with your changes.

If you lease the business, you will almost certainly have to pay the owner a percentage of your gross receipts.

Buying an Existing Restaurant

In addition to buying a space, leasing a space, or leasing a business, a fourth option exists: buying an operating restaurant. In this instance, you buy a going concern rather like leasing one. But unlike leasing a running business, you gain more freedom in the running of the establishment. Plus, you build equity in the business.

This is a particularly good option if you have found a business that you like and can see being successful, given your own improvements. In the enthusiasm of finding a business to buy, you may be tempted to ignore some of the hard realities faced by the existing restaurant. Now is the time to move cautiously, to ask questions and evaluate the answers you are given.

Begin by finding out whether the business you want is for sale. Perhaps you had a casual conversation with the owner, who let on that he or she was tired of the business and really wanted to sell and move away. Or perhaps you got the tip from an employee that the business was for sale. Don't rely on either as absolute truth. Check with the owner again and try to discover an asking price. If the owner hasn't really thought about it, you may find yourself having to do a great sell job, possibly with no results.

Once you find out the asking price, try to evaluate whether it is fair. Do your market study, finding out as much as you can about the business, the neighborhood, potential for growth, and so on (see page 23). What's the site like, how many other businesses are there? How long has this restaurant been in business? Does the local gossip consistently tell you anything of possible use? What's happening in the area?

If your results are satisfactory, try exploring avenues of financing (see Chapter 6). If the price still seems reasonable, or within bargaining distance, contact the owner or your realtor and ask for detailed information about the business.

Information you will want to find out concerns the profitability and the condition of the business, both in terms of operations and the building. Does the owner want to sell because she wants to move to a sunnier clime or because business has dropped off badly the last year or two? Looking at the books and accounts is essential here, and they should be made freely available to you or your accountant. Don't hesitate to hire a pro to examine the financial records if you are not expert in translating them.

You will want to see certified year-end sales-and-operating statements for the previous three to five years, which have been prepared by an accountant. You should also be given a balance sheet and record of sales for the current year.

The owner should provide you with bank statements and references from suppliers. Presumably an owner will give you references only for those purveyors with whom he or she is on good terms. Still, by asking questions, you can determine how much business is done with these suppliers, what quality goods they deliver, and if they are the sort of businesses with which you would like to deal.

The owner should give you an accounting of any equipment, furnishings, supplies, china, glassware, silver, and linen that come with the deal, and what condition they are in. You will probably want to check the condition yourself, but a call or visit to the company that services the equipment may also be in order.

The owner should also provide you with an accounting (preliminary at this point) of the food and liquor that will come with the business. In general, it's a good idea not to buy the extra inventory of food and liquor. Unless it's all newly purchased, much of what's sitting around is likely to be old, substandard, or not something that you will be likely to use.

You will need to know if the liquor license, if any, is included in the sale. This can be an expensive and time-consuming item to obtain if you have to reapply after the sale.

In some areas it's a matter of public record if a restaurant has violated health requirements. In other places it is not, in which case you will want to make discreet inquiries. After all, you don't want to alert the health department unnecessarily.

As with leasing and buying the space outright, you will need to know the condition of the building. This includes the conditions of the electrical wiring, plumbing, heating, ventilation, and air-conditioning (HVAC), insulation, and pest control. Do they all meet code requirements? Could you add on or change systems in the future without facing a major problem?

Making the Deal

If you are satisfied with the information you receive and collect on your own, it's time to begin negotiations. You may well want to begin with an offering price, somewhere below the asking price.

To determine your offering price, you must consider the fair market value of the restaurant in conjunction with its projected earnings. Unless you have experience in restaurant management, you may want to contact an accountant with restaurant experience or a restaurant consultant to help you understand this equation.

Your accountant or consultant may be better able to evaluate some of the information provided. For instance, are the sales realistic? Could profits have been made smaller to avoid paying taxes, or increased to make the sale more attractive? Your adviser will also know if the ratio of the costs to sales are within national standards.

Other questions concern the payroll. Does it include the owner's salary or draw? If the payroll seems too high, could it be padded or does it just reflect an expensive labor market? What is the relation of cost of food to sales?

Other costs should be checked as well, including insurance rates, utility costs, and repairs. If the insurance rates seem particularly high, some investigation into the reason might be in order. Could there be a fire hazard? Higher-than-average utility costs might indicate inefficient use of power from worn or outmoded equipment, leaky plumbing, or a poorly insulated building. If equipment repair costs are high and their incidence frequent, you can assume that some or all of the equipment needs replacement.

Other business expenses will also need to be examined. What is the overhead, the cost of employee benefits such as health insurance, and vacation pay?

For accounting purposes, you also need to know exactly which current assets come with the sale. What's the value of the fixed assets? Furnishings should be valued at 50 percent of cost if they are in good order. If they are brand new, they would be valued at 100 percent. How much equipment has been replaced or upgraded in the last year? Have any capital improvements been made? Are the taxes likely to remain the same or increase substantially? How are any mortgages, notes, or liens to be handled in the transaction?

After all the elements have been carefully considered and their importance weighed, the final question to be answered can only be considered by you. How much is the business worth to you?

One way to determine this, aside from purely emotional approaches, is to ask yourself what the business would be worth if you had built it from scratch. Take the information you've gathered and compile a list of the assets and their value. Add a fair selling profit (ask other business people or your counsel in order to determine a fair selling profit in your area), and a small amount called a goodwill factor, which allows for the business being up and running with steady customers. That will produce some idea of the business's worth.

You must weigh that value, along with what price you think you can afford and what you project the business can make. There's no one magic answer, of course. Consider the issue from as many angles as possible, work through it with your financial advisers, and come up with a price you can afford.

Once you have your offering price in mind, you can begin serious negotiations with the seller. This is where the fun begins for people who like to barter. You begin with your offering price, which may well be a little lower than you are actually willing to pay. The seller will likely counter with a price lower than the original asking price. You go back and forth, each side compromising on certain points until a deal is reached. Of course, your first offer may be accepted, which makes things much easier.

However you choose to negotiate, be sure you are represented by a lawyer experienced in the ways of restaurant real estate. A good lawyer will make sure that you are protected. For instance, a time limit on the offer should be in place so that the seller cannot keep you dangling while looking for a better offer. A noncompetition clause should be included as well, in which the seller agrees not to open the same kind of restaurant within a certain radius of the restaurant to be sold (you don't want all the regulars to follow him to his new place of business).

Making the Place Your Own

Whether you lease or buy an existing restaurant, it's often a good idea to change the concept significantly in order to start afresh.

A favorite casual stopping place of mine is called Hickory Bill's (the barbecue joint in a dining car discussed on pages 35–37).

It used to be a Vietnamese restaurant called the Dragon. Before the Vietnamese restaurant, it had been a standard diner of the "greasy spoon" variety. In its last two incarnations (the Dragon became so popular, its owners built a new, larger restaurant a mile or so away) the concepts had been so different that there was no chance of confusing them. There's little doubt that erasing the memory of what came before helped make the subsequent businesses successful.

Something of the same transformation occurred when Diane and Donald Selby bought their building for Hail Columbia. Up till then it was a seedy bar and café known as the Inn Between. For ninety years before that, it had been a meat market, housing a ladies' academy upstairs. Now it is a stylish restaurant that makes the most of its Victorian architecture.

Once you've studied your market, scouted your location, and decided on your real-estate options, you should begin thinking seriously about creating a business plan and getting financing. Then you will really be on the way toward realizing your dream.

CHAPTER

5

Creating a Business Plan

Before you spend your first nickel on a down payment for your restaurant space, you should have a business plan or prospectus in place.

A thorough business plan takes into account every aspect of the proposed restaurant that can be developed in advance. It is thus useful as a planning tool for you and as a selling tool for securing financing (as discussed in Chapter 6).

Such a plan outlines your entire business from the concept of the restaurant through your reasons for opening it. It incorporates a wealth of information including your market analysis, profit projections, and even a proposed menu with sample recipes.

Putting together a thorough proposal will help you determine your costs (both onetime and ongoing). It will enable you to assess what you can afford as well how much you will need to secure in loans. It will also help you establish goals for what the business can (or must) generate in order to stay in the black.

This is also the time to be planning your business structure, which should be included in your plan. Do you want partners, and if so, what kind? Will you incorporate?

Of course, much of the actual costs and the eventual income cannot be known in advance, but by projecting likely costs, you can create a useful plan that in the coming months may save you time and money—and possibly even your business.

Putting It on Paper

You may think you know every detail of what your proposed restaurant will be like, having planned it in your head for months or years. Maybe you've talked about it incessantly, but you still need to write it all down, to create a prospectus.

There's something about enthusiasm translated to the black and white of pen and paper that tends to refocus one's thinking. Certain things that seemed consistent or clear in your mind may not seem that way when written down. Also, having a clear outline in hand can be a great help when you go to borrow money or look for partners and investors.

Such an outline or business proposal should begin by covering a few basic areas of concern, including why you think your restaurant can succeed, what need it fulfills in the area, and how you plan to fill this need. Condense the information you've gathered and put it into clearly written form.

If you can, make the plan as attractive as possible—"sexy," as Gary Goldberg calls it—by including as much as you can about the experience your restaurant will provide. Describe your vision of the restaurant, its location, and its clientele. Include the information from your market analysis, using any valuable demographic information you may have gleaned. Try to portray what your proposed market likes to eat and how much they have to spend. Provide a sample menu with a few recipes that look so good that potential investors can almost taste them. You might even discuss how these recipes will be presented and what the decor and ambience will provide.

You will need to describe the kind of restaurant it is to be and why you want to open it. What need do you see being met by this establishment that other restaurants miss?

Any assertions you make should be supported by facts, if at all possible. If you've always wanted to open a pizza joint and there is none in town, the real-life circumstances support you. But if your town already has five, perhaps you should rethink your choice or the location.

Perhaps you plan to open a gourmet restaurant, because you haven't been able to find a really good place to eat within a fifty-mile radius. That would seem to address a need—but you should also look at possible reasons why there are no high-quality restaurants around. Can the local economy support your dream restaurant?

Next, list the reasons your restaurant will succeed. Now is the time to be clear-eyed and precise. Be confident in your expectations, but also try to be realistic. Perhaps you will be filling a real need in your area, you've found a fabulous location, your area is growing and needs more restaurants, your projected overhead is low, your concept is imaginative with a sound menu, you have a wide range of experience in running restaurants and can claim a number of other qualities for your plan. Be positive, but be honest: if the setting isn't quite right, if the local population seems to be on the wane because of plant closings, and you're not really confident that a third French bistro is just what the community needs, admit it to yourself sooner rather than later.

Once you've got the concept clearly focused, describe your chosen location and discuss why it will be the best spot for your restaurant. This is the time to view the location squarely, putting aside the excitement of having found a space. If you have hard information, discuss the terms of the lease and the requirements of the landlord.

You will next need to address the question of how long it will take to open the business. You will need to include cost estimates (preferably real estimates from contractors, lawyers, insurance agents, and anyone else involved in setting up your business). You will need to create a timetable (which may well be revised several times as things progress) that considers as many of the elements of the complicated business of setting up as possible.

When figuring time estimates, you should also be considering for yourself how you will manage the time. Will you be overseeing every aspect of the development? Will you be using a restaurant consultant? How much time and money of your own can you spend on the project before opening? Should you keep your current job to have some income?

One restaurateur looks back on her restaurant launching ruefully. She sees now that she should have kept working in another restaurant during the renovation phase of her new place. She would then have had a steady income to help support the unexpected costs, and had a little cushion when she did open. Also, she figures that the more exposure she could have had in another restaurant, the more she could have spread the word about the new restaurant. It's a good lesson.

PLANNING THE PROSPECTUS

In assembling your prospectus, address all of the following key issues. Each is important to you: as the proprietor of the proposed restaurant, you'll need to decide upon approaches or find solutions in each instance. And these considerations are among the key ones that will concern any investor or banker.

The points to be considered include:

1. Concept development (see page 14)
2. Location selection (see page 23)
3. Lease negotiation (see page 55)
4. Investment proposal and financing (see pages 65, 89)
5. Company incorporation (see page 84)
6. Insurance coverage (see page 99)

7. Menu formulation (see page 119)
8. Marketing plan development (see page 66)
9. Design and equipment specifications (see page 103)
10. Construction (see page 109)
11. Systems and accounting setup (see page 146)
12. Banking arranged (see page 92)
13. Suppliers contracted (see page 136)
14. Equipment and furnishings selected (see page 160)
15. Hiring (see page 184)
16. Staff training (see page 196)
17. Opening (see page 206)

Determining Your Costs

Almost anyone will tell you it's impossible to have too much money to open a restaurant. It seems as if no matter how much financing you get, all the dollars will somehow be spent. Perhaps even on some of the necessities.

Up-front costs will almost surely include remodeling an existing location (or building one) and the furnishings and equipment. These are areas in which you can spend just as much as you have, and then a whole lot more.

Long-term costs are those continuing costs that, no matter what, you will have to cover each week, month, or quarter. These include salaries, supplies, mortgage or rent, utilities, insurance, and taxes. And a laundry list of other costs that vary from place to place.

Start-up costs. Unless you begin with a turnkey operation (one that is already set up and going, with you just walking in to take over) it is almost impossible to know exactly how much it will cost you to set up in business. You will have to estimate, and then add extra to cover unforeseen costs and increases.

Start-up costs come under four basic groupings: development; renovation or construction; equipment and furnishings; preoperating costs.

When planning a restaurant, it is easy to forget the areas that are not directly related to the restaurant itself (such as construction, staff, and menu). One often overlooked cost is that of legal advice and its accompanying fees, although if you negotiate a lease, buy the building or land, incorporate the business, or create a partners' agreement, you will need the services of a lawyer at some point.

Unless you start out with the most modest of establishments and a clear understanding of tax law, you will probably require the services of an accountant, too. If you have the wherewithal, you may well want to call on the expertise of a restaurant consultant. You will probably want to be aware of the costs of researching your business, which may include travel, meals out, and testing. You will also need the services of a graphic designer and printer to create menus, signs, business cards, and advertising. Office equipment and supplies should be budgeted as well.

As the development aspects of the business take shape you will also most likely be faced with the costs of renovations or construction. This is usually the biggest area of preoperating expense, and you should budget as generously as you can for it. Such expenses may include the services of an architect and general contractor as well as electricians, plumbers, carpenters, masons, and tilers. Most of these services require a significant outlay for materials as well. You will also need to figure in the costs for permits, insurance, extra labor, and sundries —all the small things that you hadn't counted on and that always crop up. And then there are the inspectors (plumbing, building, electrical, and board of health).

Once your space has been whipped into physical shape, it will need to be equipped. This is another area of considerable cost. You may well need to buy kitchen equipment, including major appliances and smalls like the pots, pans, and utensils. You'll need furnishings for the front of the house, including such basics as tables and chairs, service stations, cutlery, china and glassware, a bar system, cash register, and a sound system.

Other investments may be required in draperies, carpeting, and decorative items such as flowers or art. You will need a sign, maybe more than one.

Ongoing costs. Once you've gotten the place together, you must have money available to pay for services and goods that will be covered by operating income once the establishment is up and running. You've got to have your manager, if you have one, and your chef, cooks, waiting staff, and any other help in place before opening day, and they will need to be paid. The manager and chef in particular may be involved in the preliminary operations weeks or months before opening day, and must be paid throughout that time.

You will need to stock inventory, which, until you are open, may require an up-front cash outlay. Inventory may include linens as well as foodstuffs. You'll want to keep as little inventory in stock as possible until opening, but you can't have everything arrive the day you welcome the public.

As soon as the utilities are connected, you will be responsible for paying for them. This may be months before you actually begin to bring in custom.

You will need insurance coverage before opening. The types of insurance needed in advance of opening may be different from what is needed once you're up and running. For instance, during renovation you may need construction liability insurance, which you won't need later on, but will have to be replaced by client liability.

Even before you open, you may need to budget for the costs of advertising and promotion. Your restaurant's opening can serve as an event around which to target a campaign. This will need to be planned and paid for in advance.

Last, but certainly not least, you will need a cash reserve, or float, to pay salaries and bills for the first two to three months after opening as the business builds its clientele.

All of these areas should be covered in your business plan or prospectus. You don't necessarily need to mention every single item, but the plan should demonstrate that consideration has been given to these areas and that you have allocated a certain budget of time and money for them.

LET'S TALK BUSINESS TALK

In dealing with bankers, accountants, and the bean counters of the world, you are best off if you can speak a bit of the jargon on which they depend. Be familiar with these terms:

Start-up costs: These are the bills you have to pay up-front, in advance of opening the doors: renovation costs, new equipment, furnishings, and your research. The four basic categories of start-up costs are development; renovation or construction; equipment and furnishings; preoperating costs.

Ongoing costs: These are the expenses that you will have to pay to keep going, the long-term expenditures for salaries, supplies, mortgage or rent, utilities, insurance, and taxes.

Cost of sales: In setting up a financial statement, whether a pro forma, sample statement for purposes of your prospectus (see page 73) or the monthly profit-or-loss statement you'll need to monitor ongoing business (see page 82), there are certain financial terms that you should be familiar with. One is cost of sales.

In any business, cost of sales refers to those ongoing costs for the goods needed to make your product. In your restaurant, this means the food and beverage supplies you purchase. Typically, cost of sales runs about 36 percent of your gross receipts.

Gross receipts: This number is your total sales, namely the total number of dollars and cents you collect in a specified period.

Operating expenses: Operating expenses include payroll, linen, utilities, cleaning and maintenance, insurance, taxes, and other miscellaneous expenses. Industry averages vary from one part of the country to another (and you should find what it is in your area), but 41 percent is a commonly used average.

Real-estate expenses: Rent, real-estate taxes and insurance, and amortization of improvements to the property (namely, that loan you took to remodel the place) all belong under this heading. Try to use a real cost in budgeting, but 6 percent is pretty typical.

Overhead: This is a catchall term that is variously defined from business to business. In the food service business, it generally refers to operating and real-estate expenses.

Debt service: This is another commonly used financial term: it refers to your monthly expense for any loans or mortgages your business is carrying.

Depreciation: The IRS allows you to deduct a certain percentage of the dollars you have invested in equipment, since it gets less valuable the more you use it. Consult your accountant to determine what is reasonable; 1 or 2 percent of your gross is a typical percentage.

Profit: And now we come to the good news: after the expenses are paid, from food to the help to taxes to your greedy landlord, the rest is yours.

Creating a Pro Forma Statement

One way to help predict the success of your business is to create a pro forma statement or sample financial statement, an essential part of your business plan. This document outlines the anticipated sales and expenses over a given period, usually a year.

A pro forma, while only a projection, is useful when you go to apply for financing (see Chapter 6). Anyone willing to lend you money, from a bank to a venture capitalist, will insist on seeing such a prepared financial statement.

If you have restaurant experience, so much the better, because you will have a body of information on which to draw. If you don't, you will have some homework to do in pulling the figures together. Luckily, national averages exist for some of the budget items you need to calculate. The Small Business Administration and the National Restaurant Association keep current records of averages for such factors as rents, salaries, financing, and guest checks, all of which they will send you on request.

It is easiest to start a pro forma statement with predicted expenses rather than sales. Begin with those that can be accurately determined, such as rent or debt service and insurance. Expenses such as food and beverages can be predicted using national averages, adjusted for your area. You can determine costs such as payroll using calculations of average salaries for competing restaurants in your area. By adding all the possible costs together, you will be able to see how much money you will need to make in sales in order to survive.

Expenses to be determined for a pro forma statement:

- Food and beverages
- Rent or mortgage
- Property taxes
- Insurance
- Utilities
- Payroll
- Building and grounds maintenance
- Equipment maintenance and repair
- Laundry
- Linen replacement
- Uniform costs should you provide them
- Tableware, china, and cutlery replacement
- Paper and cleaning supplies

Profit, sales costs, and sales are the last elements to be entered on a pro forma statement. You need the estimated costs for the above-mentioned items in order to determine these figures. As a very rough guideline you can figure that payroll will constitute about 28 percent of your operating budget. Other operating expenses usually run around 19 percent. Occupancy costs average about 6 percent and depreciation of equipment usually takes another 1 to 2 percent.

SOURCES OF INFORMATION

In assembling the information you need to get under way—whether you're looking for industry averages for your model financial statements or other kinds of advice and assistance, some of the following sources may prove invaluable to you. Don't hesitate to seek them out.

National Restaurant Association
Educational Foundation
250 South Wacker Drive
Chicago, IL 60606
(312) 715-1010

This organization can provide general information regarding the restaurant industry nationwide, but even more important can refer you to state and local restaurant associations.

National Institute for the Foodservice Industry
20 North Wacker Drive
Chicago, IL 60606
(312) 782-1703

Both of the above groups can provide information regarding cooking-school programs nationwide and their certifications. Some schools offer programs ranging from vocational certificates to postgraduate degrees.

The Guide to Cooking Schools
Shaw Associates
625 Biltmore Way, Suite 1406
Coral Gables, FL 33134
(305) 446-8888

This annual publication lists cooking schools nationwide.

Public Restaurants and Institutions
1350 East Touhy
Des Plaines, IL 60018
(708) 635-8800

Restaurant Business
Bill Communications
633 Third Avenue
New York, NY 10017
(212) 986-4800

Nation's Restaurant News
LeHar-Friedman, Inc.
305 Madison Avenue, Suite 535
New York, NY 10165
(212) 371-9400

These three publications are trade organs for the restaurant business. You may find a wide variety of information available within their pages.

SAMPLE FINANCIAL STATEMENT

Name of Restaurant: *Your Place*
Forecast Year: 1991

	Cost in Dollars	Percent of Total Sales
Total Sales		
Food	$175,000	70%
Beverages	$ 75,000	30%
Total	$250,000	100%

Cost of Sales		
Food	$ 62,500	25%
Beverages	$ 27,500	11%
Total	$ 90,000	36%
Gross Profit	$160,000	64%
Operating Expenses		
Payroll	$ 70,000	28%
Other	$ 47,500	19%
Total	$117,500	47%
Gross Profit Less Operating Expenses	$ 42,500	17%
Real-Estate Expenses		
Rent	$ 10,000	4%
Taxes	$ 1,250	0.5%
Insurance	$ 1,250	0.5%
Amortization of Improvements	$ 2,500	1%
Total	$ 15,000	6%
Profit Less Real-Estate Expenses	$ 27,500	11%
Depreciation	$ 2,500	1%
Net Income Before Taxes	$ 25,000	10%

Forecasting Sales

In addition to evaluating your proposed costs, you will also need to project how much money you can expect to bring in.

To determine this, you will need to consider several factors that, as yet, may not exist.

First, you will need to figure about how many meals you can serve each day. To do this, begin by figuring the number of proposed seats in the restaurant (taking into account space for passage, tables, kitchen, operating areas, and rest rooms). What meals do you plan to serve: breakfast, lunch, and dinner? breakfast and lunch? or lunch and dinner? Then you need to figure how many meals you will be likely to serve each table from the kitchen.

How many days each year do you plan to be open? Are you likely to have a busy season, followed by a slow one? Finally, take the cost of the proposed average check and multiply it by the proposed number of meals served per year.

Let's create an imaginary example. (Compare this process with the pro forma statement on page 76, for a more complete listing of the numbers in this example.) We'll say your ski resort restaurant will be open for dinner only, from five until ten o'clock, six nights a week, four months of the year, or 133 nights. Most tables will turn three times in the course of the evening, but those that seat six or eight only turn twice. We'll say some of the tables turn three times and some twice for an average of two and a half times each dinner period.

Your restaurant will seat fifty people, for 125 meals each night. Say the average guest check will be around twenty-five dollars per meal. Multiply the number of meals served each day by the number served each year by the average cost per check to reach the projected amount of sales for the first year. Thus, you come up with 133 business days × 125 daily meals × $25 per guest check, producing a gross of $415,625.

This figure is not a real figure, of course, but shows what you might be able to earn. In real life you will have to figure that some nights and times of year will be better than others. (Your market research should have given you an idea of such fluctuations; in our hypothetical example, Christmas is in there, and February vacation; but the snowfall is quite unpredictable.) For that you may want to create another figure showing a more modest, less-than-full-house estimate. Let's say the lower figure will project a 60-percent occupancy or seventy-five meals per night. This produces another calculation: 133 × 75 × $25 = $249,375. Let's round it off to an even $250,000.

FIGURING THE AVERAGE GUEST CHECK

In order to project sales, you have to have a figure that represents an average of the cost of meals served. To do this, you have to know what kind of food you will be serving and its rough retail cost.

You may think that most of the meals you will serve will run around twenty dollars per person, but you must remember that some people will order only salad and an appetizer, and some might come in just for dessert and coffee. Your figure therefore would have to be scaled down to account for this.

Once you're open or if you are already working in a restaurant, the easiest way to figure the average check is to take the receipts for a given period and divide this total by the number of customers served. This can serve as a useful method for checking your projections, but is not possible in advance of opening.

On the other hand, one way to start in advance of your actual opening is to use industry averages for various types of restaurants. These approximations are as follows:

- Fast-food restaurants generally run around five dollars per check.
- Breakfast-and-lunch counters average around six dollars.
- Family dinner restaurants average about eight dollars.
- Bar bistros around fifteen dollars.
- Fine restaurants range from thirty to well over one hundred dollars.

Again, these are averages, and therefore are subject to regional variation and changes due to inflation and other factors. You might do best to determine what typical checks are at your model restaurant, if you have one, but the above averages may be helpful for your pro forma calculations.

Creating a Profit-and-Loss Statement

In addition to a pro forma or sample financial statement, which is used to project possible earnings and probable expenses, you will need to create a monthly profit-and-loss statement, also known as an operating statement, as a way of monitoring your expenses and income.

This statement is set up much as the pro forma is, and it includes much of the same information, including sales, cost of sales, operating expenses, real-estate expenses, depreciation, and profit. The purpose of the operating statement is to track monthly figures and to compare them to your budgeted and previous month-to-month figures.

Sales. Daily sales figures are usually kept in a sales register or journal. Columns are set up for food, beverages (often wine and liquor are broken out individually), and miscellaneous. Some states require separate breakdowns for cigarettes and beer, should you sell them. Sales tax must be entered as well.

Cost of sales. Determining the cost of sales is crucial to the operating statement because it tells you how much was used during the operating period. To figure a very rough estimate of cost of sales, many people assume that it is made up of the monthly purchases. A more accurate measure is to use an inventory system.

An inventory system can be helpful to you in managing your business in a number of ways. For one, a monthly check of your goods disciplines you to monitor your purchases, revealing which items are used most frequently and which don't seem to move at all. That tells you something about your customers' tastes, seasonal changes, and other fluctuations that you may wish to consider when selecting menu items.

Second, comparing the value of goods used against what you have in store is the only true way to determine your cost of sales.

Third, by keeping a close accounting of your stock, you will be able to order proper quantities at the most opportune times. The last thing you want is to have extra food hanging around for prolonged periods. Even if the food doesn't spoil, it costs you to have that excess inventory sitting in your storeroom. Finally, conducting a monthly inventory helps to cut down on the amount of pilfering you are likely to encounter. (For more about creating an inventory system, see Chapter 9.)

To figure the true cost of sales, you compare the inventory on the first day of the month with what you were carrying on the closing day. Subtract the closing number from the opening number, and be sure to add in the cost of any purchases for that month. Subtract the cost of any credits, and the resulting figure will be your cost of goods.

Operating expenses. Your monthly profit-and-loss statement will include your actual operating expenses. These expenses are directly related to sales.

Operating expenses include payroll expenses (wages, payroll taxes such as Social Security, unemployment insurance, Workmen's Compensation), utilities, hauling and waste removal, laundry, cleaning, credit-card compensation, supplies (office and kitchen), utensils, licenses and permits, professional fees (accountant, lawyer), insurance, repairs and maintenance, bank and finance charges, debt service, dues and subscriptions, advertising, and any other regular expenses that come up in the course of several months of operating.

Real-estate expenses. These costs are not affected by your sales, but are fixed. They include rent, mortgage payments, depreciation of equipment, insurance outside of operating, corporate administration, leasehold improvements (if applicable), and real-estate taxes.

MONTHLY PROFIT-AND-LOSS STATEMENT

Name of Restaurant: *Your Place*
Month of Operations: January 1992

	Cost in Dollars	Percent of Total Sales
Total Sales		
Food	$ 45,000	66%
Beverages	$ 23,000	34%
Total	$ 68,000	100%
Cost of Sales		
Food	$ 17,000	25%
Beverages	$ 9,000	13%
Total	$ 26,000	38%
Gross Profit	$ 42,000	61%
Operating Expenses		
Payroll	$ 15,000	22%
Other	$ 13,000	19%
Total	$ 28,000	41%
Gross Profit Less Operating Expenses	$ 14,000	20%
Real-Estate Expenses		
Rent	$ 2,500	4%
Taxes	$ 600	0.6%
Insurance	$ 425	0.4%
Amortization of Improvements	$ 625	1%
Total	$ 4,150	6%

Profit Less Real-Estate Expenses	$ 9,850	14%
Depreciation	$ 1,350	2%
Net Income Before Taxes	$ 8,500	12%

Business Structures

As you plan your business, you will need to consider the kind of structure within which your business will be run. Do you want to be the sole owner, have partners, or incorporate the business? How you structure the business will determine, in part, the kind of financing you can expect (see Chapter 6) as well as the way your business operates.

Proprietorship. The easiest way to start your business is to keep it simple, and for you to be sole owner or "proprietor."

In a proprietorship, you are responsible for everything. All profits become your personal income, and are taxed as such under IRS provisions for the self-employed. The assets are all yours, as are the liabilities. If the business thrives, you need not share the profits with anyone, and if it fails, you are personally responsible for the losses. If someone files suit against the restaurant, you will be held liable. If the business fails, creditors can levy charges against your personal assets in addition to those of the business, including your house. You take the risks, reap the profits, and have full control over your business.

Partnership. When two or more people agree to go into business and to share in the profits, it is known as a partnership. Partnerships have to be registered with state or local authorities.

It's a good idea to have a formal document drawn up by a lawyer outlining the duties and contributions of each member of the partnership. Indeed, in some states it is mandatory in order to meet statutory requirements.

Creating a partnership is one of the standard ways of getting private financing and in sharing of profits. Some members of partnerships contribute labor or abilities instead of money, others money only. Generally, all reap the rewards of success and all share in the liabilities, just like a proprietorship. Partnerships do not dissolve on the death of a member, unless no heirs survive.

Kinds of partners. "Active partners" are those who work in the business and may have contributed money. "Silent partners" usually contribute money, and often expertise, but they are not actively involved in the business. A "limited partner" initially contributes money but assumes no liability and has no control over the operation of the business. An "ostensible partner" is one whose name and credit are used in the business but who has no financial interest.

Your lawyer can advise you on the best way to set up your partnership, should you choose to go this route, in order to conform with the Uniform Partnership Act that has been adopted by most states.

When drawing up a partnership agreement your lawyer should cover a number of essential points. These include:

- Contribution of each partner, be it time, money, expertise, whatever
- Duties of each partner
- Signing officers of the partnership
- Distribution of profits, liabilities for losses
- Voting arrangement
- Method of departure from firm for partners
- Actions of the firm to be taken on the death of a partner

When it comes to taxes, a partnership is treated much the same as a proprietorship. Each member files a personal tax return showing the proportionate loss or gain that resulted from the partnership.

Corporation. Incorporating your business into a company

with limited liability is the most expensive form of ownership, but also the safest. An incorporated company is considered a legal entity. The corporation is responsible for the debts and liabilities of the company—you personally, as a stockholder, are not held responsible.

Corporations are chartered by states. Certain formalities exist to forming a corporation, and they vary from state to state. Generally you need two or more people to form a corporation and these people hold offices, including president, vice-president, secretary, and treasurer. Many states allow people to hold more than one office. It can be as simple as you and your spouse or you and a partner. Some states require that you have an attorney, known as a solicitor for the purposes of incorporation, and that you hold an annual meeting.

Taxes are filed for the company, rather than as part of an individual's income. You will have to pay both state and federal income tax on any profits the corporation makes. Whether you make money or not, you need to file tax forms annually.

There are a number of advantages to incorporating. The principal one is in limiting the liability for which you will be responsible. Your liability will be limited to the amount of money you invested in buying shares in the corporation. If the company fails or if someone sues the company for damages, the company owes the money, not you. There are exceptions, however, should you provide personal guarantees to suppliers, banks, or landlord. You will be personally responsible to them in the case of failure.

Since the corporation is a separate entity, of which you may be the principal shareholder, you can be an employee as well as an owner, taking a salary from the corporation apart from any profits that may result. This means that you can claim certain expenses and fringe benefits.

When your business is incorporated, you can easily bring other people into the company, by selling shares. This is one way to invest employees in the business with profit sharing.

There are a few downside elements to incorporating. In the first place, the paperwork for incorporating can be more expensive than that for a partnership. Second, since corporations are chartered by the state and must file income tax returns, they can be more closely regulated by the government. This is rarely a problem for a well-run business, however. Finally, record keeping, accounting, and legal requirements are somewhat more complicated for a company than for an individual.

You should ask your attorney to brief you on the pluses and minuses for your particular situation.

The complexity of having partners. Many partnerships work extremely well. However, be aware that bringing anyone into your business, whether as a partner or investor, or a member of a corporation, can be risky.

Diane and Donald Selby of Hail Columbia vowed never to have partners again after their first restaurant venture in California. They started out there with someone who came in as a working rather than an investing partner. One of his jobs was to handle the finances.

"He just took all the money to the bank every night," Diane recalls. "Only the bank was home." Three months after opening, the other partner left town, taking the money with him. Only then did the Selbys discover that none of the suppliers had ever been paid.

In contrast, many partnerships and corporate entities work well. Sherry Delamarter is co-owner with four other people of four successful restaurants in New York City (see page 32), and they function as a collective. Almost without exception, no one is allowed to own stock who has not put in "sweat equity" by waiting tables, cooking, or hauling garbage. They have resisted outside investors in the belief that most outside investors are not interested in dealing with the unglamorous daily operations but are very happy to demand perquisites. "Those are the kind of owners that will call up a manager on a Friday night and say, 'I'm sending over twenty people,' when they have no place to accommodate them. They aren't there for the customer."

Then again, the investors can bring important custom to a restaurant. At TriBeCa Grill, also in Manhattan, the group of celebrity investors, including Robert De Niro, Bill Murray,

Sean Penn, and Christopher Walken, got the restaurant into the gossip columns for months in advance, and the place has been packed since opening, despite delays and problems. One of the wise decisions made at the TriBeCa Grill is also worth remembering: a successful and skilled restaurateur—Drew Nieporent, owner of Montrachet—was made managing partner.

If you choose to use investors, be sure that they know that you are in charge, that they are investing in your abilities to make a successful restaurant. Also be sure that you have a controlling interest in the stock.

Once you've got your plan, including the business plan or prospectus, the pro forma statement, and your business structure, it's time to think about securing financing.

CHAPTER

Financing, Taxes, the Law, and Insurance

Once you have targeted your market, found a suitable location, and completed the rest of your restaurant plan, it's time to create a real live business.

This is one area where the carefully constructed business plan you've compiled stands to pay off. It can help secure financing, the process of which we will discuss shortly. Once you have the money lined up, you will probably need permits, licenses, and anything else that your municipality requires to make your business legal. Those, too, are the subjects of this chapter, along with setting up a tax structure and protecting yourself and your investment with insurance.

All of these steps can seem daunting, but you don't need to have an MBA degree to complete them (on the other hand, a course in small-business management might prove very useful). These steps may also seem dull and boring if you are fired with a passion for the more creative aspects of restaurateurship. Yet unless you are blessed with a levelheaded business partner willing to take on the tasks for you, they are all necessary and important in making your business venture successful.

Finding Funding

One of the biggest hurdles you face when trying to start a restaurant is raising the money to get started. The more experience you have in the industry, particularly working in or managing successful operations, the more likely you are to succeed in getting what you need. This doesn't mean that if it's your first time out, you should give up now.

Having created a business plan (see Chapter 5), you will already know how much money you need and how much you can expect to make in sales for your first year. With this information in hand, you can begin to approach various sources for the capital you need.

Where do you begin, and what can you expect?

When thinking about where to start, it may help you to understand that there are two basic kinds of capital: equity capital and debt capital. Equity capital is money that you personally provide the business, and that you stand to lose. Such money includes personal savings, inheritances, cashed-in insurance policies, and monetary gifts from friends and relatives.

Debt capital is money you obtain from an institution such as a bank, finance company, government agency, or even the current owner, based on the strength of the business prospects.

Equity capital. Equity capital is more risky from a personal standpoint than debt capital. You cannot declare bankruptcy and expect your savings account to be reimbursed or your house mortgage to be paid or your friends and relatives to earn back their investments. However, it is sometimes the only kind of money people starting out can raise.

Personal assets. Many people who decide to open restaurants have been planning and saving for years. You may have bank savings, securities, or real-estate investments that you can draw upon for necessary cash. Even if you have a mortgage on a real-estate holding you may be able to draw on its equity through an equity loan or second mortgage.

Unless you have a corporate backer, you will probably find that most institutions willing to loan you money will insist that you put some of your own money into the business. If the business becomes profitable, you will reap the benefits most directly if your money has funded it; however, if only losses result, you will have lost your own money, and possibly that of your friends and family. For these reasons, you might wish to pursue all other avenues of raising money first, as discussed below.

The least risky form of personal asset is inherited money. Of course, we all wish we were born with the proverbial silver spoon and with a freedom never to have to worry about paying bills. Few of us have that luxury, but a surprising number of people find that a relative has left them a little nest egg. Even if the sum is not huge, it may be enough to seed a growing business. As with your own savings, you don't have to worry about making interest or principal payments on inherited money.

Friends and relatives. Using private assets is risky from a personal standpoint as well. Nothing strains relations more quickly or intensely than issues of money. If you choose to draw upon such assets, particularly loans from friends and relatives, be sure to arrange the loans in a businesslike manner. Draw up papers stating the loan repayment schedule with any interest you negotiate with the lender. With friends and relatives your payback may not be on as strict a schedule as it would be with a certified lending institution, but in one form or another you generally will be able to reimburse your investors.

Real-estate assets. If you don't have cash savings, you may be able to raise money from a real-estate asset. Depending on how much equity you have in the property, you may be able to take a mortgage on real estate you own and use the money for the business. Of course, you will be paying monthly costs on the loan for years to come, and you risk losing the asset should the business not thrive.

Maria and Guy Reuge, owners of Mirabelle, a fine small restaurant in St. James, New York, used a novel approach to raise private financing. Guy is a great chef, and Maria was an editor at *Gourmet* magazine, and they planned their restaurant around his food.

To raise money to buy the house they had spotted and convert it into a restaurant they held a series of fund-raising dinners for prospective investors. It was not a quick and easy way to get the money, as it took them many dinners and a lot of convincing, but it worked. And so has the restaurant, which is recognized as one of the finest establishments on Long Island and does a solid business.

A young couple in Santa Fe, New Mexico, weren't quite so lucky in their financing. After being turned down by several banks, they got some—but not quite enough—financial help from a few small investors. Well into the process, they found themselves about $40,000 short of what they needed to complete their renovation and get things going, and at last had to rely on family financing to open their long-anticipated restaurant.

It was the husband's mother back in California who actually mortgaged her house to help with the unexpected increase in costs. They finally opened, but within six months closed the restaurant—business just wasn't good enough. But today, nearly five years later, they are still paying the monthly costs, which they will continue doing for many years to come. They'll both tell you it's a very risky gamble to start a restaurant; but in nearly the same breath they'll wax enthusiastic about the new venture they are planning in San Francisco.

Life insurance. Life insurance is another avenue to explore when trying to scare up equity capital. Many people carry life-insurance policies that have loan value. Term policies do not have such value, but others do. The cash value on many policies is available to you to borrow at a low interest rate. The larger the policy, and the longer you've held it, the more cash value it has. Your insurance agent should be able to advise you about borrowing against your policy.

Debt capital. Finding someone else to help bankroll you in your new venture is far preferable to going into hock yourself or risking loved ones' savings. However, because you are asking a third party, usually an institution, to lend you money, it's likely to be harder to secure such loans.

In general, lenders want to be guaranteed a return on their investment. This is where your business plan will be of particular use. If you can prove that you have already planned the restaurant carefully and can show with reasonable certainty that the business will survive and prosper, you are more likely to find investors. If you have a body of experience in the industry, this will help enormously as well—particularly if you've been involved in successful ventures—by lending credibility to your claims of knowing what you're doing.

Bank loans. The obvious place to start looking for money is from a bank. Banks are the most logical places to go for money, as they are generally secure and regulated. However, they are also conservative investors since they must protect the interests of their depositors. Back in the days of the savings-and-loan boom, you might have had an easier time securing a loan, but today banks are ever more wary of possibly unsound investments—and restaurants are known as particularly bad risks, since the failure rate is so high.

Once again, this doesn't mean you shouldn't try to get a bank loan. You may be able to convince a commercial bank to loan you the money you need. But before you apply for a bank loan, be sure you are thoroughly prepared.

The bank will require a number of documents, including your business plan or prospectus with a pro forma or sample financial statement, a statement of financial net worth, a résumé, and any other pertinent documentation you may have. The bank may require that you provide as security the assets of the business, your personal guarantee, or your personal assets (home, car, or securities). A third-party guarantee or a combination of the above may also be requested.

A third-party guarantee usually means that the bank wants you to have someone cosign the loan. Finding a cosigner can be difficult, since that person becomes responsible for the money, should the business default.

You should also be aware that your statement of net worth

will be discounted by as much as 25 to 50 percent. This is to allow for the reduced yield the bank would realize should it have to seize your assets and sell them quickly.

If the bank turns you down for a loan—be assured that if it happens, it will be for business reasons only—ask them why. They will often be happy to tell you, and this information can be useful when applying to other banks or lending sources.

Supposing the banks do fail to lend you the money you need, there are other options. Some of the traditional ones are cited below, but you may also want to get a little creative, as Frank Tortoriello did.

When The Deli in Great Barrington, Massachusetts, recently lost its lease, owner Tortoriello found that local banks in the recession-plagued area were unwilling to help finance a move. He printed his own "money" and enlisted the aid of the community. The scrip—called "Deli Dollars"—were worth ten dollars in food; Tortoriello sold them to his customers for *nine* dollars. The Deli Dollars were redeemable six months after purchase, giving Tortoriello his much needed short-term loan.

The Deli Dollars sold out within days of being issued.

Some of the more usual approaches are these:

Small Business Administration. If a bank has turned you down, you might try contacting the Small Business Administration, an agency of the federal government designed to help small businesses. Some businesses have found these agencies frustrating to deal with, but they can be useful, particularly when it comes to guaranteeing a bank loan. Occasionally, they will participate with a local bank in lending money, and sometimes they lend money directly under their Economic Opportunity Loan Program. Contact the Small Business Administration for current information and requirements regarding their services.

Small-business investment companies. SBICs are licensed by the Small Business Administration to provide loans. They operate independently, but you can obtain a listing through your local SBA office.

Housing and Urban Development. Occasionally the federal government's HUD will provide loans to restore and rehabilitate buildings in certain areas. They will not finance a business, but if you have a building that needs work, you might consider contacting your local HUD office. If they deem it worthy, they might provide some renovation funds that could defer some of your up-front costs in preparing the space.

Current owner. You may be able to apply to the current owner of the property you wish to buy for financing. This kind of transaction is often handled like a mortgage, wherein you pay a percentage of the total down—often 30 percent—and then amortize the principal plus interest over periodic installments.

Sometimes such owner financing is done for the real estate only, other times for the business as a whole should it be a functioning restaurant. This method works best when you buy a complete business that needs little overhauling. If you need to remodel or renovate, you will need additional financing.

Landlord. Even if you're leasing a space, you will probably need money for renovations. Occasionally, the landlord of a building will provide financing for leasehold improvements. He or she will probably want a portion of your sales in return. There are several possible ways such a deal may be negotiated, but often a straight loan arrangement is made.

Credit union. Credit unions were founded in many cities by citizens, union members, or other groups interested in helping one another. If you already belong to a credit union, you may be able to arrange a loan through it. The process will be very similar to applying to a bank, and the more thorough and convincing you can be in the presentation of your business plan and personal finances, the more likely you are to find help.

Finance company. You may turn to a finance company for money. They do make loans to small businesses, but beware that they usually charge high interest rates. Loans often mature much more quickly, as well, meaning you have less time to pay them off. Don't go to a finance company for a large or long-term loan, as you will probably find yourself paying rates that might, in the end, damage your ability to turn a profit.

Venture capital companies or investors. Venture capitalists are people willing to finance risky investments such as restaurants. Often they are individuals with extra money who like to live their financial lives a bit dangerously in the prospect of a large return.

Sometimes they form companies and invest professionally. Venture capitalists typically take a large percentage in ownership of a business in which they invest. They may be silent or not, but more often than not they protect themselves by having a significant say in the running of a business in order to protect their investment.

Be careful when investing with venture capitalists to make sure that you maintain control over the running of your business. On the upside, such companies and people often have valuable business experience and can, as a result, be useful partners.

TIPS ON OBTAINING A LOAN

1. Shop around for the best terms available and apply to those sources first.
2. Try to get your loan commitment arranged before negotiating for your restaurant or space.
3. Be sure to get any loan commitment in writing.
4. Never sign a loan agreement without first having it reviewed by your accountant or lawyer.
5. Be sure that any loan you take out can be prepaid without penalty.
6. Make sure that any construction loan you take out requires you to pay interest only on the commitment as you use it.

Financing Goods

Financing can take many forms, and you may well wish to employ several methods. When it comes to actual goods such as equipment and supplies, some companies offer their own financing. You may wish to investigate such a route.

Equipment. Restaurant-equipment-company financing plans can be straightforward financing with interest payments or they may take the form of leasing with an option to buy the equipment at the end of the lease. Some companies simply rent equipment. Service is often part of any such deal, either as part of the package or under a separate service contract.

Sales representatives may put together a package of equipment at a special price for which you pay monthly installments. If you go with such a plan, be sure that you need all the equipment in the package, and that you can buy the equipment after a certain time. You may also be able to lease equipment economically so that at no time are you responsible for the full costs of replacement. Generally speaking, however, the best deals on equipment are made by directly purchasing only what you need. When it's time to replace a piece, it will still have some worth with which you can bargain for a new piece.

Suppliers. At one time, food purveyors commonly provided goods and equipment essentially on loan in order to create a market for their products. They helped the buyer, and the buyer agreed to buy exclusively from them. This method has, in some cases, evolved into franchising, and many franchisors provide financing to prospective buyers directly or through a finance company. If applicable to your business, you may wish to explore this approach.

Taxes

Finding the prescribed path through the maze of tax regulations can be very confusing and time-consuming. Hiring an accountant familiar with current business tax requirements to help set up a tax structure is often the easiest and, in the end, most economical way of dealing with the complex demands of the various tax requirements you will face.

The following are the kinds of taxes with which you will soon become familiar.

Federal. Once you start a business, you must begin paying the federal government. To begin, you have to file for an employer identification number, through your local Internal Revenue Service office. The government will then send you the appropriate forms as you will need them.

An employer is responsible for collecting taxes from employees and paying them to the government. These include Social Security and income taxes, which must be paid monthly. In addition, you will be required to match the amount of Social Security you collect from employees on wages earned.

You will be required to provide your employees with a year-end tax form known as a W-2, which states how much money was made over the year and how much was withheld for various taxes. All employees, whether they still work for you or not, who made more than six hundred dollars during the year must be sent a W-2 form.

Depending on the size of your operation, you may be required to pay federal unemployment tax on a quarterly basis. If you do, you also must file a specific form at the end of the year.

You also cannot forget your income taxes in discussing the federal government's requirements. Throughout the year you will be paying income tax and at the end of the year filing your own personal-income-tax forms, in addition to any for a partnership or corporation.

Your local IRS office should be able to provide you with useful booklets describing the rules and forms needed in order to comply with current laws.

State. The federal government will no doubt require the largest tax payments, but the state gets a good share, too. You will be required to pay income tax, probably personal as well as business, state unemployment tax, and to collect sales tax if one is levied in your state (and/or city).

The requirements for collecting sales tax vary from state to state. Some states don't require it to be collected on served meals, but do on carryout meals or liquor. Some states require that you break the different categories out: food, liquor, beer, and cigarettes, should you sell them. Your county or state capital building is generally a good place to start in determining what paperwork and payments are required.

Local. Municipalities often get their share of taxes as well. These often include income and occupational wage taxes, which you must deduct from employee wages. You also may have to pay property taxes. Some cities collect a business tax as well. Inquire at city hall as to what payments will be due and when.

Licenses and Permits

The array of licenses and permits required when opening a new restaurant can be bewildering. They may range from operating licenses such as liquor to onetime permits for construction. Before you start the work of getting your restaurant in shape to open, contact your local government to discover what kinds of licenses and permits you will need to proceed.

Liquor license. In most states, if you plan to serve liquor, your right to do so will have to be established by a state authority and a local authority, and it will have to be filed with the federal government. The manner in which liquor licenses are awarded varies from state to state and town to town.

It can be as easy as applying and paying the fee and waiting a short while for the license to come through. In some places it can be very difficult and expensive to obtain a liquor license. In some areas getting a license to sell only wine and beer is considerably easier than a full liquor license. Certain restaurateurs have found the whole process such a hassle that they have opted to serve no alcoholic beverages; some of them allow patrons to bring their own. And, of course, some counties allow no alcohol to be served whatever.

Permits. Your local government will require you to have operating permits. These generally include one from the health department certifying that the restaurant is clean and that food is handled properly, and one from the fire department showing that you meet the fire regulations to ensure the safety of patrons. Your town may require others as well.

In addition to operating permits, if you do any sort of renovating of the space apart from replacing appliances and painting, you will probably have to have permits for work done, followed by inspections. Don't be surprised if you need permits for any and all electrical work, plumbing, and construction.

Regulations. Most municipalities and states have their own laws and regulations regarding the running of restaurants. Most of them involve the sanitary preparation of food. Some have to do with employee working conditions. Still others have a bearing on customer convenience and accessibility.

Your local health department, fire department, and building department should be able to inform you of the regulations you will need to follow. Since regulations and laws change frequently, it's a good idea to join a local restaurant association or become active in local government. That way you can be kept informed about pending changes and sensitivities in the community.

Insurance

As a business, your restaurant will need to be as fully covered against such disasters as fire, theft, and lawsuits as possible. You simply cannot afford to lose your investment due to a fire, or to someone's claim of negligence after a fall suffered in your parking lot, or worse yet, as the result of illness from contaminated food.

You will need to balance having enough coverage to feel safe, but not so much that the payments seriously erode your restaurant's profitability. Deciding the kinds and levels of insurance needed takes some planning and research into what's available and at what cost. Call around to insurance agencies in your area and interview those specializing in business insurance.

The following are the primary kinds of insurance you may need.

Fire and extended coverage. This type of insurance covers you for damage done to your building and contents due to fire, natural disasters, and vandalism. Try to insure for 100 percent of the value of the property and equipment (you likely will be required to insure for 80 percent, anyway), since replacement always costs more than the initial outlay. Most insurance companies will approve a policy only after one of their loss-control engineers has inspected the property to be sure that it meets their codes and requirements for a safe building.

Liability. Liability insurance is fast becoming a vital part of operating any business, most particularly restaurants. Coverage comes in three forms. General liability insurance protects you against injury to someone on your property. This does not cover working employees, who are covered under Workmen's Compensation, but customers or other outsiders. Product liability insurance covers you in case someone becomes ill as a result of eating the food.

Liquor liability. The issue of liquor liability has been intensely argued in recent years, as more states have passed laws making the person who serves liquor responsible for accidents or crimes committed by intoxicated people.

Liquor liability coverage can protect your business in the event of a suit. Buying this coverage makes particularly good sense if you intend to do a lot of bar business. Unfortunately, the more bar business you plan to do, the harder it is to get coverage, because of the increased risk. The rates and accessibility of liquor coverage depend on the percentage of your business that is liquor. Highly rated insurance companies are most apt to cover you if liquor sales constitute 25 to 30 percent or less of your business.

Auto liability. If your business owns a car or truck for delivery or picking up of goods, you would be liable if an employee was injured while using it. As a result, your business should also carry suitable car or truck insurance, as applicable.

Theft insurance. If your business is to be located in a high-crime area, you might want to consider a policy to cover losses due to breaking and entering.

All of these kinds of insurance should be discussed with the insurance agents you interview. They will provide you with a bid based on a package of insurance policies. Of those listed above, the absolute necessities include fire and extended coverage and comprehensive liability. The others can be added or not as you deem fit. In addition, you might want to discuss an umbrella policy for additional liability; a fidelity bond to cover dishonest employees; and business-interruption insurance to reimburse you for sales lost due to a disaster to the business such as fire (or even a power outage, as one insurance agent told me was the case with a restaurant she insured in New York City). These are generally not as important, and can be expensive.

Fringe Benefits

The following forms of insurance are considered fringe benefits for employees. The restaurant business is not generally known for its generous fringe-benefits policies, but you may find it to your advantage to invest in some of them, particularly if you wish to develop a loyal employee pool.

Medical insurance. Increasingly, the restaurant business provides access to medical insurance coverage for employees. This often takes the form of the employer and employee sharing the costs for the employee in a group plan. This is known as a contributory plan. The insurance company then pays a portion or all of the health-care costs due to injury or illness for an employee or family member.

Dental insurance. This kind of coverage, found mostly in large corporations, pays for dental care for an employee or family members.

Retirement. A retirement fund is a useful fringe benefit for those employees who are with you over a long period. Most young people who work in the restaurant business as a stopgap while waiting for something else (whether they ever move on or not) don't find the notion of a retirement plan very interesting. Some other employees do, particularly older employees.

Contributions to a retirement fund usually begin after an employee has been with you for a certain period, usually several years or more. Such funds can be contributory or noncontributory, in which you pay all the costs. Retirement funds can be set up so that the employee may or may not, depending upon the plan, remove the money from the fund when he or she leaves your employ before retirement.

Life insurance. Some employers provide life insurance to employees as a benefit. Life insurance pays a beneficiary a set amount should the employee die. The employer generally pays the cost of premiums.

Key-person insurance is a form of life insurance that insures the life of an owner of a corporation. If he or she dies, the corporation is paid as beneficiary and can use the money to buy the owner's stock in the corporation.

Now you've gotten financing. Or you're in the process of securing it. You've set up a tax structure, applied for permits, and investigated your insurance needs.

Your business is really taking shape. Now that you know about certain key business considerations, it's time to begin planning the spaces in which you will be entertaining your patrons.

CHAPTER 7

Shaping the Space

Having chosen and arranged for the purchase or lease of the space, it's time to begin the process of making it your own. This may entail touching up the paint and purchasing some new flowers; at the opposite extreme, you may need to build a new structure or renovate an existing one.

Unless yours is a turnkey operation, however, you will probably be faced with a certain amount of renovation. How much you do depends on a variety of factors, including what the space was most recently used for, whether you own or lease, how large a budget you have, and what you are trying to achieve.

Generally speaking, it makes little sense to spend a great deal of money remodeling a rental space. If you must rent and you feel it is necessary to spend significant amounts of money on renovating the space, try to secure a long-term lease so you can recoup your investment over a longer term. In rare instances, landlords can be convinced to share in part of the cost of repair and remodeling; it probably won't hurt to ask.

If you own the space, you are free to do anything you want within local laws and restrictions. On the other hand, for many people the cost of buying the building limits the monies available for renovations. Such are the common trade-offs.

For some people the physical image of the restaurant is as or more important than the food to be served. The notion is that people will come to the restaurant for the total experience, and that the food is not as important as the atmosphere. Sometimes economic factors intervene as well, as in cases where the atmosphere and decor are so expensive that the food has to be compromised in order for the restaurant to break even or make money.

These days the public demands more out of restaurants. It's often no longer enough to eat in a pretty restaurant, but the food must be good, too. This is not to say that plenty of successful restaurants aren't known primarily for their architecture or decoration.

Chef and restaurateur Bruce Marder has a talent for creating provocative restaurants. He is credited with being the first on the West Coast to hang the paintings of local artists on the walls of his West Beach Café in Venice, California, thus transforming a bare room into a showplace. At another of his restaurants, Rebecca's, also in Venice, he hired the architect Frank Gehry, known for his flamboyant designs (including some of the imaginative new buildings at Disney World in Florida), to transform the restaurant, which serves upscale Mexican food, into a Jules Verne underwater fantasy.

He located another glamorous restaurant in Santa Monica, and called it DC3, after the much-beloved 1930s transport plane that made commercial aviation viable (see page 40). The restaurant is located adjacent to the Museum of Flying and actually one story above a real DC3. Marder hired the artist Charles Arnoldi to create a decor that is an imaginative floating space station. For Bruce Marder it is important that his restaurants have a most distinctive style, regardless of the cost.

Most people, however, don't have unlimited funds or a market that needs a flamboyantly designed restaurant. But they do need to have a space made into an efficient and attractive restaurant. How do you go about taking your space and turning it into your restaurant?

For Sherry Delamarter the atmosphere of her restaurants is decidedly idiosyncratic. At the Cowgirl Hall of Fame in Greenwich Village in New York (see page 32), the walls are covered with western memorabilia, including posters, place mats, ashtrays, and postcards. One showpiece of the establishment, tucked away in a corridor, is a collection of barbed-wire under Plexiglas. The lighting consists of wall sconces that have photographic shades of cowgirl events and reunions.

At Tortilla Flats, another of Delamarter's successful restaurants, the narrow space is decorated with Christmas lights, fake-wood paneling, and black velvet paintings of Elvis.

On the Upper West Side of New York, Bahama Mama, a very casual Caribbean-style restaurant, features colorful three-dimensional paper fruits and birds hanging from the ceiling as the main decorative element, along with bright murals of island scenes.

If you're like most people who are enthused about opening a restaurant, you probably have a mental vision of the total picture—from the food served to the art on the walls. That vision is important, as the clearer the idea in your mind, the better.

Yet you may still need the services of professionals in the field, including an architect, restaurant designer, contractor, and possibly a restaurant consultant. You may need one, some, or all of them. It all depends on your needs and your budget.

Do You Need an Architect?

Depending on the amount of work to be done, you may or may not need the services of an architect. If your renovation needs are simple, you have a clear vision of just what you want and need, and you have a good design sense, you can probably get along without one. If your needs are elaborate and your budget generous, you will probably want to shop around for one.

There are several methods for finding a good architect for your job. Perhaps the easiest is to find a restaurant with a look you particularly like. You may well have run across one while doing your market research. Try to find out who the owner used. This is a good way to get a reference, too. You want to know before hiring an architect whether he or she managed the job on schedule or caused lengthy delays.

Another method for finding an architect is to ask people you know who have had commercial work done and who were pleased with the work. This should give you a list with which to begin your search. Search through design magazines for ideas; call up these magazines and ask for architects in your area, as they often keep listings.

If you still don't have many leads, check with other professionals in the field. If you know any contractors, they can be great sources (so long as you remember that contractors and architects, almost by definition, don't get along). Real-estate brokers and bankers are other possible sources. You can also write to the American Institute of Architects (1735 New York Avenue, NW, Washington, DC 20006, or your state office) for a listing of licensed architects in your area. Even easier, check the Yellow Pages of your phone book (although not all architects will be listed) or your local Better Business Bureau.

Once you've made up a list of several promising candidates, make appointments to meet with each one individually. Once there, outline your needs and budget. Try to get a sense of the architect both professionally and personally, and be sure to see other restaurant work that's been done. Restaurant consultant Gary Goldberg suggests that if the architect fails to ask two questions, he or she should be ruled out immediately. These are: Who is your market? and what is your menu? The design of your restaurant must match your clientele and your food.

Many restaurants are designed before their owners have decided on the market and menu. This almost guarantees disaster. Gary tells of one restaurant in New York in which the food, the architecture, and the service just didn't mingle. A very talented chef produced very formal French food, but the restaurant was stark and the service casual. The elements didn't work, and the patrons didn't come, despite the brilliant food.

Before you leave the architect's office, get a list of references. Once home, call the references and ask questions such as: Was the architect flexible to your needs and wants? How smoothly did the job go? How well did the architect work with the contractor?

Once you've chosen your architect, the next step is to work with him or her to get what you need. Perhaps the most important thing is to have a clear understanding between the two of you from the outset. You will need to establish a working rapport, which is much easier if you've chosen someone you like. The more information you can provide about your needs and wants, the better, too. Be sure also that you establish a fee schedule with clearly delineated responsibilities early on, as this will save you from future misunderstandings. You should be sure you understand the cost of developing a design and working drawings, the cost of changes, and where costs can escalate further along in the project.

Once you've hired your architect and given him or her your charge, the next step is to review preliminary plans. This is when you can walk away (having paid the sum for the drawings and time involved) if you find that the two of you will never see eye to eye. If you like the preliminary plans, proceed to final plans and construction.

You may choose not to work with an architect. In all likelihood you will still need plans drawn up from which other crews will work. Indeed, your town may require you to file drawings before any work can begin. If you are a talented draftsman, you may be able to draw mechanical plans such as for carpentry, plumbing, and electrical work yourself. However, if you're not, it's best to hire a draftsman to make plans for you, or to leave it to your contractor, who can probably take care of them.

Working With a Restaurant Designer

Assuming you don't need an architect to manage major renovations or structural changes, you might elect to use the services of a restaurant designer, a person whose profession is developing the efficient layout and decor of a restaurant. Restaurant designers are adept at knowing the best uses of space. They are interior decorators, taking an idea and creating a total look for you. Their services can be quite expensive, but if you have a substantial budget, a restaurant designer can be a worthwhile expense.

How do you go about finding a restaurant designer? As with an architect, your market research may have led you to restaurants that you especially liked. Ask the owners of these establishments who they used and if they were satisfied with the work. Were their instructions followed, all local codes met, and the job done on time and within budget? If this route brings you no luck, try contacting local trade or business associations and design magazines.

The process of hiring a designer is very similar to that of hiring an architect. You will need to establish a good working relationship in which your ideas and wishes are taken seriously and followed whenever possible. You will want to see sketches at various points in the process and be a part of all decisions. The fee schedule will need to be agreed on before work starts.

The designer will require you to provide information as well. The more information you can provide about your wishes and needs the better. Such areas include the menu and market, style of service, amount and kind of space, and location, to name just a few. Designers are accustomed to providing detailed information regarding space needed for each function of the restaurant as well as matters of equipment, furnishings, and decor. You may choose to have the designer lay out the kitchen, although most people find that it's best left to those who use it, namely the chef or cooks and owner.

Working With a General Contractor

If you are very handy or experienced in the building trades, you can arrange and oversee all the work that needs to be done. If not, you will need to work with a general contractor whose job it is to coordinate your project, and to hire and oversee the work of subcontractors.

A contractor may do some of the work personally or with an in-house crew—general contractors are often also carpenters—but hire out some or all other jobs such as plumbing and electrical work. In other words, a contractor takes your plans (and sometimes can even arrange to have plans drawn) and carries them through the whole process—in return for payment. It is thus essential that you have a contractor who is reliable and trustworthy. Even then, you must be able to keep track of progress and, if necessary, hold costs in line.

The procedure for finding a reliable contractor is similar to that of finding an architect. Many states and municipalities require that general contractors be licensed. You can check with your local Better Business Bureau for the names of licensed contractors. You should also ask around. Local building-supply houses often know which contractors pay their bills on time and work to schedule. If you use an architect, he or she may have someone who is especially good. Other restaurant owners who have had work done may offer leads as well. The best of all possible approaches is to use someone you've used before and whose work you have liked. This is not always possible, however.

Diane and Don Selby of Hail Columbia in Chatham, New York, hired someone whose work they knew to convert the bar they had bought into a restaurant. He promised to work quickly over the winter, since he had no other work pending. Other jobs came in, however, and their job was pushed further and further back, and the costs began to rise. In the end, their opening was delayed six months (past the crucial summer season) and the costs tripled from the original estimate.

One of the Selbys' strongest pieces of advice regarding the

hiring of a contractor is to make sure you hire on a fee basis. Most contractors make a bid based on a percentage (usually 10 to 30) of the estimated time and materials required to do the job. This should be agreed on in advance, with penalties in your contract for overruns of time and materials. You should also be sure you understand what changes will cost in advance. Payment should be tied to performance.

When hiring a general contractor, follow some of the same steps as for hiring an architect. Make a list, meet with them all, outline your needs (including schedule and budget), and assess whether you can develop a working relationship with someone.

If your budget allows, try to choose someone with a range of experience in restaurant work. That can help make sure your job is done efficiently and within budget. If you are on a very tight budget, you may do well with someone who is just starting out but who has skills and is enthusiastic and organized. Your restaurant may provide the showcase that someone starting out needs. The same holds true for architects.

Being Your Own General Contractor

Since opening a restaurant is in large part acting as a general contractor for a variety of services and goods, you may decide to act as your own general construction contractor as well. All it takes is time, patience, skills with people, finance, and general good sense for you to be able to save quite a bit on the costs—usually around 20 percent. You also retain control, since you can be sure that all the jobs get done exactly as you want them.

There are important elements to weigh when making a decision. If you're not familiar with all the subcontractors available in your area for specific jobs, it may take you considerably more time and energy to find good people (and to coordinate their work) than it would take an experienced contractor. You also have to be a good manager of people, getting them to take your job as a priority over others, making sure that work is done to specifications and on time and budget. You will be responsible for paying the subcontractors directly.

Finally, being your own general contractor can take quite a bit of time, which you just may not have, given all the other demands on your time when opening a restaurant.

Designing the Working Spaces

Even if you hire experts to create and carry out plans for renovating, remodeling, or building your restaurant, the better you understand your needs, the more satisfied you will be with the end product.

How do you start planning your space? Take everything into consideration: receiving, storage, food preparation, cooking area, sanitation, dishwashing, service, dining area, rest rooms, and parking. Within each area, decisions must be made regarding the type of equipment and where it will go—where booths and tables will be placed, and what layout will best facilitate service. Even if you take over an operating restaurant, you might want to improve the placement of appliances and work stations. Each area of the restaurant must be considered carefully.

The efficient kitchen. A well-planned kitchen can make the difference between a thriving operation and a struggling restaurant. You have to have the customers to keep the place busy, of course, but if you cannot serve them efficiently and quickly, then they may not return for the all-important second, third, and fourth visits.

Planning a kitchen to meet your needs is not all that difficult. If you hire a restaurant consultant, he or she may make suggestions that you find particularly useful. Similarly, an architect experienced in restaurant design may be able to advise you. You can even garner advice from restaurant supply representatives. For the general layout, however, if you have a little common sense, you can design the kitchen yourself.

The most important thing to keep in mind at the outset is that everything in your restaurant must be geared toward serving each meal quickly and efficiently. The experience of dining in your restaurant may be leisurely—but it shouldn't take forty-five minutes for an order to leave the kitchen.

To begin, you have to think of the kitchen as the workhorse of your operation. It may not be terribly large, but it must be efficiently arranged. From the moment an order enters the kitchen it enters an assembly line, beginning with the raw materials and ending with the "plated" meal. If that assembly line becomes sidetracked and has to stop, reverse, and move sideways before resuming its forward progression, something is amiss.

Each area of the kitchen—cooking, food assembly, and dishwashing—should be self-sufficient but interactive. This means that the materials and equipment to cook the food should be in one area, logically laid out and easily reached. The area where the food is assembled—this often includes cold dishes, desserts, and salad—should be near the cooking area, but not so that its operation interferes. The dishwashing area will need to be discrete from the cooking and preparation areas (and as far from the dining room as possible), but accessible so that clean dishes can be delivered as necessary.

In order to think through the process clearly and to determine the most efficient flow of traffic and goods, begin by spending time in the kitchen or proposed kitchen. Walk through each of the processes. Ideally, you want to create a loop of movement, through which little effort is wasted. The waiting staff enter the kitchen, where they drop off orders with the cooks and dirty dishes with the dishwashers. When food is ready, cold preparations are picked up first, followed by the hot items. Then it's out the door to the dining room.

Each of these areas must be planned to accommodate the particular duties performed. The main areas include the cold-food preparation area (often used for advance preparation as well), cooking area(s), dishwashing, and storage.

Cold-preparation area. In most full-service restaurants, the average meal consists of an appetizer or salad, or both, before the entrée, and then dessert. If yours is this kind of establishment, you will need a cold-food-preparation area.

It should have a counter with enough space for advance preparation work, which can be cleared away before mealtimes and the assembly of dishes. You will need space to house the equipment and ingredients for each of the dishes to be composed. You will also need room under or over the counter for plates, bowls, and other necessary equipment. Basic utensils for serving and assembling will also need to be housed.

In examining the kitchen, do you see an out-of-the-way place fairly near the entrance at which these dishes could be prepared? If the area must double as the advance-food-preparation area, it will need to be near the cooking area. Will the waiting staff be serving up salads and adding dressings? If so, is there a station, even out of the kitchen if space is tight, where that can be done so that it doesn't interfere with other operations?

The cooking station. The chef or cook's work area may be the most important station in the kitchen. It, like all the others, must be designed to be efficient. You will have to try to envision exactly what needs to be done here. Walking through the preparation of dishes is one helpful way to achieve this. This depends, of course, on the kind of food you will be serving: Will your kitchen rely on the broiler and burners for sautéing? Will you be serving foods mostly from a grill? Will you be specializing in slow-cooked dishes from your oven and stove?

Whatever methods you will be using, start with the moment an order is delivered. Somehow the chef will need to see the order. Will orders be arranged on an eye-level carousel, or on a bar above the assembly counter? What comes next?

Let's take this possible scenario as an example. An order for sautéed chicken breast with mushrooms and lingonberry sauce has just been placed in front of the chef, along with three other orders for the table. The chef must heat a pan with butter, take the chicken from refrigeration, dredge it in seasoned flour, add the chicken to the heated pan, sauté it, add mushrooms, continue to sauté, leave the pan to cook for a few moments while beginning another dish, come back to it, turn the chicken, continue with the next dish, come back to it, remove the chicken from the pan and arrange on the plate, add a little seasoned broth to deglaze the pan, stir, turn to prepare next dish, turn back to the pan, swirl, add a spoonful of already prepared lingonberry sauce, swirl the pan to incorporate and heat, pour over the chicken, garnish with vegetables, and finally set the plate aside for the waiting staff to pick up when the table's other three meals are finished.

Clearly, everything will need to be at hand, with little or no walking from station to station. There must be pans available to cook in, butter next to the stove to dip into, chicken ready to be cooked within reach, utensils for cooking, flour next to the refrigerated chicken, sauce within reach, vegetables, either cooked or parcooked, within reach for final finishing and plating. There must be a supply of plates at hand, preferably warm, and utensils for handling the food.

Try going through such exercises in each section of the kitchen, keeping in mind that everything must be accessible. For instance, the dishwashing area must be discrete from the cooking and food preparation area, but it must be accessible enough that dishes can be restocked in the preparation areas. The dishwashing area must also be accessible to the busing staff.

In addition to the service areas of the restaurant, you will also need to consider accommodations for delivery and storage. If at all possible, deliveries should be made from a back door near the kitchen rather than through the restaurant. If you can, it's also helpful to have bulk food storage and clean laundry stored fairly near the delivery area as well.

The dishwashing area. The area where dishes and pots and pans are washed should be away from the constant flow of traffic but close enough to the workings of the kitchen that dishes and pots and pans can be easily reached and replaced. Many restaurants try to have a drop-off area near enough to the door from the dining room that dirty dishes can be deposited easily, without having to traipse through the other kitchen stations, yet not so close that the noise of dishwashing intrudes into the dining room.

Most health departments require that you have separate sinks for washing and sanitizing pots and pans and dishes. In all likelihood you will be using an automatic dishwasher for the dishes, glassware, and silver that goes into the dining room, as well as for some small kitchen utensils. For the majority of kitchenware—pots, pans, and utensils—you will have someone scrubbing by hand.

The health department may also require a certain configuration of your pot sink. The most common is a heavy-gauge stainless-steel sink with three compartments and a drain board at each end. These come in a variety of sizes.

Food storage. You will need space for both short- and long-term storage of foodstuffs. Most municipalities have regulations regarding food storage, and you must find out what your local laws are before deciding that, for instance, all the canned goods will be stored in the basement. In any case, the ideal kind of storage is that which is easily accessible for delivery, out of the way of the everyday rush, but within easy reach.

You will probably try to work out an arrangement whereby large quantities of some foods such as staples and canned goods can be stored in a back room near the back door (ideal as far as delivery is concerned, but not necessarily good if you happen to have light-fingered employees), in the basement or loft, and others are kept near at hand. Finding space for the items that need to be kept nearby can be difficult if space is tight.

Your local health code may also determine the frequency and kind of vermin control you must have. This may affect your storage capacity and arrangement. Pest control is a continuing part of the maintenance of every restaurant. For this reason, you will probably need to have your staples stored so that they can be easily moved out of the way of regular spraying or inspection.

Coordinating staff action. The methods by which your serving and cooking staff coordinate their actions is vital to the efficiency of the kitchen. The most important of these is the communication between the cooks and waiting staff.

Orders must be placed so that the cooks can see them and evaluate their order of preparation. There are several devices to achieve this. One is a rack with clips placed at eye level on which the server attaches each order. Another is a carousel equipped with clips that the chef scans and can move around to check other orders. Sometimes the server hands in the order and the chef or assistant picks it up and places it in the most convenient spot available.

Equally important as the placement of the orders is the placement of the plate for the server to pick up, and the signaling of its readiness. Some places use a pass-through or open window from the kitchen area to the serving area. Plates are placed in the window as they come up from the chef. Sometimes the server's name is called when the order is ready.

The chef's work area may be topped by a shelf on which the server picks up the order. Sometimes the server has an assigned portion of the shelf where the order is placed once it's ready. Some establishments use numbers to indicate when an order is ready. In a small restaurant, the staff is often so well coordinated that the servers know how many minutes after their orders have been placed the dishes will be ready and waiting. They check at the appropriate time, find their orders waiting, check them over for accuracy, and proceed to the dining room.

WORK AREAS OF THE KITCHEN

In planning your kitchen, you should consider the performance of these tasks:

Premeal preparation:
Cooking and mealtime assembly
Specialized food preparation
Side-dish assembly
Dessert preparation and service
Baking and/or bread making
Ice making

Dishwashing and pot washing
Delivery, reception, and unloading

Storage:

Walk-in, cold and frozen foods
Counter warming
Dry storage
Clean linen
Dirty linen

Miscellaneous:

Office area
Staff personal space

The Dining Room

Designing the dining room is much more a matter of personal taste and style than laying out a kitchen, and one in which you may wish to let your architect, designer, or consultant have more of a free hand than you would with a kitchen. Whatever method you choose to use—hiring out, doing it yourself, or not changing a thing—you should plan out the basic flow of traffic.

You will need to plan from two perspectives, that of the customer and that of the working staff. The needs of both will have to be met. The customer will need to be able to move freely and easily within the space and be seated with enough room to be comfortable.

The optimum space per customer is twelve square feet. Generally, it's better to be a little cramped in a restaurant than to have a great yawning room that never looks full unless every single seat is taken. Studies have demonstrated that people are less intimidated by being slightly crowded than having too much room in a restaurant. However, this is not to say you should strive to have everyone's elbows touching.

To see how the flow of traffic might move, let's begin with the customer. Pretend you are the customer. You arrive. Is there somewhere to hang your coat? Is there a station at which to check in, or will someone be there to meet you?

How do you find a seat? Are seats easy to reach? Is there a selection of seating appropriate for different-sized groups? Will you be paying your bill at the table or at a cash register? Where is the register located? How easy is it to find the rest room? Do you have a view of the kitchen from many of the seats you might choose? Are many seats located near the service stations? How good a chance is there that the seat chosen will have a good view?

Next, pretend you are a staff member. Again, trace the movements needed to serve and clear a meal. Where do you enter the dining room from the kitchen? Are there corridors wide enough that staff members can move freely to and from the kitchen? Where are the service stations located? Is it easy to reach all the seats at every table for serving? How are the stations divided? Is the access to the service bar convenient? Does each station include some "good" tables, almost guaranteed to produce good tips and frequent turnover?

As you develop a clear arrangement in your mind for your restaurant, both food preparation and serving areas, you'll also—more or less simultaneously—need to develop your notions of the food. In the next chapter, we'll talk about that very subject: the food you'll serve and the drinks your patrons will consume.

CHAPTER

8

Food and Drink: The Heart of the Matter

What you serve at your restaurant is as important as the site, the decor, and the ambience. For most restaurateurs, it is the heart of the business.

Your menu may even be your most important means of selling your food. It attracts customers and keeps them coming. As recently as only a dozen years ago, a menu was little more than a shopping list. But today, it is a key determinant in the success or failure of every restaurant.

Most people starting out have a pretty clear idea of the kind of food they want to serve; many instinctively plan their menus after their own favorite dishes. It's often the first thing that comes to mind.

However, the first question to ask yourself when setting out to plan your menu is: what kind of food should the restaurant serve? Before you think dishes, consider categories and types of foods. Do you want plain, simple fare, or more elaborate food? Will you be working with a theme such as special ethnic food, or even a particular variety of food, such as seafood or pasta?

Whatever kind of food you envision serving, it should also meet a perceived need in the community. If there are already six salad-and-burger bars in a four-block radius, there is probably no need for a seventh. If there's an established steak house down the block that serves good meals at cheaper prices than you could ever charge, try another tack.

You must also consider the ability of local suppliers to provide the foods you need. For instance, if your dream is to open a fish restaurant in the heartland, thousands of miles from the shore, you had better be sure you can count on a reliable supply of fresh fish and seafood. You might also try to diversify your needs a bit as well, featuring the local freshwater seasonal catch as well as oceangoing standards. By doing this, you may be able to develop a following based on your special local dishes.

Some items on your menu may not be profitable, but deserve to be there nonetheless. For instance, the menu at the Routh Street Café in Dallas, a restaurant known nationally for its innovative food, features wild game of the state, including Texas axis venison and Texas Hill Country wild sheep—although the prices for those meats are thirty-five to forty-five dollars a pound wholesale. But those dishes are crucial to the image of the restaurant. According to owner Stephen Pyles, "We want to be a showcase for products from the Southwest. It makes no sense from a financial standpoint, but it's important for the reputation of the restaurant."

Similarly, at the Rainbow Room in Rockefeller Center in New York, the management is forever debating whether to take the double-cut lamb chops (thirty dollars) off the menu because they command only a 50-percent markup. However, since the dish is a signature of the restaurant, it stays.

Nuts-and-Bolts Menu Planning

When just starting out, you will need to gather as much information about the food you want to serve as possible. This includes gathering recipes, testing, costing them out, and standardizing them. You may want to leave much of the planning of the actual dishes and recipes to the chef. If you do, you should still act as adviser, making sure he or she carries out your vision. In any case, you should have a hand in the basic menu planning.

No matter what kind of menu you choose, it needs to be balanced, offering a variety of nutritious food. It need not be vast. In fact, unless you plan to open a coffee shop where the list of basic dishes seems endless, you will do much better to offer a menu that has a variety of selections but is not overwhelmingly large.

A balanced menu includes foods of different textures, colors, and types, all of which complement one another. You should have enough variety that people will want to keep coming back for their favorites and new dishes. Even if you specialize in one kind of food, you will do well to diversify a bit within the range. For instance, if you plan to open a Tex-Mex restaurant, you probably should offer the odd gringo burger for patrons interested in less spicy, more middle-of-the-road fare.

Changing times are evident on today's menus. As the costs for real estate, food, and labor increase, the already slim margin for profit narrows. This is reflected in many restaurants by fewer menu selections and fewer dishes that require costly ingredients or a lot of preparation time. Just keeping the ingredients on hand for a huge menu is very expensive both in dollar outlay and in wastage. Rare is the person who can't find anything to eat on a well-balanced and interesting menu, even if it is quite short.

Plan to serve dishes whose main ingredients can be used in more than one way. If you have a shrimp entrée, include a shrimp appetizer as well. On the other hand, there is no need to offer four kinds of poultry on a short menu, unless there is a very special reason for it.

Trying to offer too many kinds of foods on a menu is the mark of an amateur, as it unnecessarily increases your food costs and wastage. Unless your restaurant is large and does a large volume, you cannot order enough of a great variety of ingredients to get a good price, and it's difficult to use up certain foods while they are fresh.

Elaborate dishes should be balanced with a few simple ones. Not everyone who comes to your restaurant will have an enormous appetite, nor will everyone want only light foods with no sauce.

Balancing elaborate and simple dishes makes sense not only from the diner's viewpoint, but from the vantage of the kitchen staff as well. If every dish takes a great deal of preparation and final fuss, you will find your labor costs run out of hand (or the food will make it to the table very slowly). Indeed, one way to achieve a menu balanced for price as well as food is to have some dishes that are simple and quick to prepare while others are more labor-intensive.

I know of one long-gone restaurant in Stony Brook, New York, whose menu suffered severely from a lack of balance. The chef and owner was well trained and had imaginative ideas, and he produced delicious food. However, every dish on the menu was unbelievably rich. Each appetizer, salad, entrée, vegetable, or dessert contained rich ingredients, including quantities of butter and cream, often in heavy, rich sauces. By the end of the meal, everyone at the table would feel oversated, that uncomfortable sensation that accompanies too much of a good thing. Though most of his dishes were delicious, the chef was unable to build a regular clientele who made the restaurant their hangout. The food was too much to think of eating there more than occasionally.

Then, of course, there are successful restaurants that don't pretend to provide a balanced menu. If you've ever been to a beach resort, you know that fry shacks can do amazingly well. They may sell only fried clams, fish, or shrimp, maybe with a little coleslaw for vegetable. They may or may not offer places to sit, and if they do, it's often outside or in a screened porch.

Chauncey Creek in Kittery Point, Maine, is essentially a dock with lobster pound. You can order steamed lobster, lobster rolls (a sandwich), steamed clams or mussels, and that's it (except for drinks from a soda and fruit-juice machine and bags of potato chips). Anything else you bring yourself. Patrons sit at picnic tables and just concentrate on luscious steamed seafood.

If you can, try to develop a signature dish for your restaurant, something that people will remember you by, recommend to their friends, and look forward to eating when they return. This can be an entrée, or a special salad, even a giveaway appetizer. The Elm Court Inn in North Egremont, Massachusetts, has a house pâté that they serve to every table along with the bread, before orders are taken. It was so well loved by patrons that when the restaurant changed hands, it stayed as part of the drill.

The look of each plate as it leaves the kitchen is important, too. Some say it is almost as important as the taste of the food, since it provides the first impression of the meal, which influences every bite. For this reason each plate should leave the kitchen looking like a composed picture. Dishes need not be fussily prepared, looking like Vermeer still lives or the latest in minimalism. But they should be pleasing to the eye, with a balance of textures and colors.

You must also take into account the volume of meals you need to be successful. If you envision your restaurant making its profit on a large number of meals served, you will have to be sure that those meals can be produced quickly. That may mean that you will need to rely heavily on foods that can be broiled or sautéed, two very quick cooking methods. This doesn't mean that the menu need be limited to plain broiled steak. Much can be done with sauces or relishes made ahead.

At the Old Mill the policy is to keep it simple. The food is far from boring—their grilled chicken breast with corn crepe, black-bean puree, and lime salsa attests to that—but most of the entrées rely on broiling and sautéing. "You get new chefs every now and then," says owner Terry Moore, "and they want to do this and that. I tell them, 'You have to understand that we're going to do more than a thousand dinners a week, so you have to keep it simple!' The first time they get caught and orders back up, they realize they're strangling themselves."

A la Carte or Table d'Hôte?

There are two basic kinds of meals in good restaurants: à la carte, in which each dish must be ordered separately, or table d'hôte (also known as prix fixe), in which a complete meal is served for one price. With an à la carte menu you stand to make more money, since people have to order courses separately. Most restaurants these days serve meals à la carte, but there are advantages to both methods.

A la carte meals often provide side dishes. Some restaurants include bread, vegetables, and salad with the entrée, leaving the diner to buy an appetizer and dessert separately. Other restaurants charge separately for each item.

Many restaurants provide table d'hôte menus, often as a special feature, in addition to an à la carte menu. One of the advantages of the table d'hôte method is that you can plan a whole meal that balances flavors, aromas, textures, and, not to be underestimated, cost. You may provide diners with a couple of options for, say, the appetizer and the dessert while they entrust the other decisions to you.

Another benefit of the table d'hôte menu is that you can really control the meal. You can easily take advantage of market and seasonal specials knowing you will have little wastage.

Whichever method you choose to use, keep the list of side dishes fairly short. Many restaurateurs feel that providing choices for people actually adds a burden to their ordering, particularly when the list of choices is more than four or five items long. They find that most people are happy with what they are given so long as the dishes are fresh and well prepared and not too unfamiliar. If diners need to choose, it is much easier for them to specify which of two vegetables, two potato dishes, and the kind of salad dressing they prefer than to listen to a litany of a dozen or more choices. Asking any more of them is confusing. Providing more choices than that also increases your inventory and wastage.

Green salads are very popular with diners today, either as a separate order or as part of the entrée. If you include one as part of the entrée, you need not provide five different kinds of dressing, but can have a house salad with a signature dressing. If it's a good dressing, you may be delighted with how many people will be pleased with it, and how few will ask for something different. The reputation of many a restaurant has been made on the house dressing, since everyone who eats there has it. If you choose this method, you should probably keep good olive oil and vinegar handy in cruets for the particularly health-conscious patrons who want only a very small amount of the plainest of dressings.

Perhaps the most economical way to run a restaurant is to have a single menu each night. Patrons can either call up and ask the day's menu, or you can post it in the window. This usually works best with small restaurants. Table for Two in Portland, Oregon, owned by caterers Nancy Briggs and Juanita Crampton, is perhaps the smallest restaurant in the world. A set luncheon is served Tuesday through Friday—for *two people*. Located in the front parlor of a Victorian house, the restaurant opened in 1985 and was created to serve meals that would be difficult to serve to crowds—food Juanita Crampton calls "esoteric." Reservations are taken four times a year and are gone within an hour.

Perceived Value

Another critical element in planning your menu is what your diners will perceive as good value. This is crucial to the overall success of the restaurant and, like so many things, is a combination of all the elements you put together. Factors in the value assessment will include the food and its presentation, service, ambience, your attitude—in short, everything about the experience of your restaurant. Anything you can do better than the competition will work to your advantage.

When it comes to determining the value of the menu, begin by reexamining your marketing survey. You probably noted what competitive restaurants serve as part of their standard menu. For instance, if salads are included with an entrée as a matter of course in your area, you will probably need to provide one, too. If everyone in the area expects large portions, you will probably have to pay attention. Some restaurants include a free signature snack—fritters, pâté, perhaps a small cheese sampler—which can add enormously to the perceived value.

People have different expectations for the different kinds of restaurants they frequent. When they go to a very expensive restaurant, they rightfully expect a lot more from every aspect of the restaurant than if they go to a simple family-style joint. But at both, everyone has standards of value.

Menu Pricing

Pricing your menu is tricky but all-important. It involves analyzing your food and labor costs to come up with a price scheme, which you then must compare with your competition. "It all boils down to money," according to Roberto Donna, chef and part owner of Galileo and I Matti in Washington, DC. "When you are dealing with low prices and high volume, you constantly have to think about what ingredients cost and how much labor dishes entail."

It's helpful if you can start with a general range. In that range you should include foods in the high, middle, and low range. As Brian McNally, owner of five trendy restaurants in New York, says, "You've got to give people the *choice* of ordering something cheap."

As you begin pricing you will discover which of several methods works best for certain dishes. But before you begin setting prices, you should understand that the most expensive restaurants generally have low food costs but high labor costs. Inexpensive and moderately priced restaurants often have fairly high food costs, but low labor costs. Ethnic restaurants tend to have low food costs and low labor costs, and thus often low prices.

The factoring method. This approach, by which you multiply the cost of ingredients by three, used to be the standard method. It works well for mid-priced items, but doesn't work so well for low-cost dishes.

For example, if a bowl of soup costs you only thirty cents to make, you should not sell it for ninety cents. The full cost of labor cannot be included at that price, it's just too low.

Factoring doesn't work with expensive items, either. Say, for instance, you plan to include steamed lobster on your menu. Let's say the lobster costs you fifteen dollars. You can't expect, realistically, to ask forty-five dollars for it.

This method does work well for foods in the mid-range. For a grilled chicken dish, for example, with tomato dumplings and sorrel sauce, the costs of the food might come to about five dollars. You can easily charge fifteen.

Gross margin pricing. This method of pricing deals with dishes in which the cost of ingredients is high. Such would be the case with the fifteen-dollar lobster. If your restaurant is the kind that can serve a lobster dinner, you can probably charge, say thirty dollars. Your food cost is half of the menu price, meaning the gross margin, after material cost has been deducted from the menu price, is fifteen dollars on each portion. A 50-percent gross margin is a sensible financial goal when using this pricing approach.

The prime cost method. The two methods above consider only the cost of the ingredients. For some dishes that is enough, but for others that require quite a bit of preparation, you need to consider both of the main costs of running a restaurant, food *and* labor.

To determine the prime cost, add the cost of labor and the cost of food, then add a percentage for profit. If you feel you can charge the resulting amount, then you're set. Sometimes the figure, without any profit added, is prohibitively high. In these instances, you'll have to eliminate the item from the menu.

Competition pricing. This method of pricing involves taking information from your marketing study and comparing it with similar items on your menu. This method gives you a clear understanding of what your competition charges. When pricing competitively—which most every restaurant must do, at least in part—be sure to look at the whole meal. Many people will take only the cost of a similar main course and compare them. What they may neglect to include are the extras, such as side courses included.

There may be other elements to consider as well, including how long a competing restaurant has existed, and whether its proprietors own the building, or whether the operation is family run, with resulting low labor costs. You may find after you price your competition that you will have to revise your menu in order not to compete directly. You may also find that you can provide a better value than your neighbors at roughly the same price.

Gary Goldberg tells the story of a client who had built a beautiful, trendy restaurant in a seedy part of town. When they opened, they charged $2.50 for a hamburger—a price at which they couldn't make any money. When he asked the reason for such a low price, the owner responded, "Because that's what everyone else around here charges." Gary responded, "But you're not everybody else in the neighborhood." They raised the price to $4.50, yet had no problem selling their burgers.

Combination pricing. The last method of pricing is the all-of-the-above approach. Consider factoring, gross margin, prime cost, and competition approaches for different dishes, as appropriate. And try to balance the prices of the competition with your costs and needs.

Despite the importance of careful pricing and menu planning, people are occasionally successful despite a lack of careful price planning. When Sherry Delamarter and her partners opened Tortilla Flats, the first of their popular restaurants, they didn't even plan the menu or pricing.

On the night they opened, one of the partners said, "Gee, I guess we need a menu," so Sherry sat down and wrote "Taco ... $1."

"We didn't even do food costing before we started," she remembers. "We said, 'Well, that sounds like a good price for a taco.'"

Designing Menus

According to Richard Melman, founder of Lettuce Entertain You, a successful chain of twenty-eight restaurants based in Chicago, "The menu is the most important sales tool a restaurant has."

It only makes sense to make it look as attractive as it possibly can. It need not be a work of art so beautiful that the food and prices become secondary, but it should appeal to the eye and highlight the food in a pleasing manner.

There are two basic kinds of menus, those that are individual, providing one for each diner, and a "blackboard" menu in which the day's menu is written on a large board placed strategically in the dining room. Many restaurants use both, with a printed menu for the basic items that remain unchanged and a blackboard menu for the daily specials. Still others combine the two methods by listing the daily specials on a card, one or two of which are then placed on each table or clipped to each menu. A blackboard doesn't have to be like those used in school; it can be any large, easily altered form of menu that announces to entering patrons and to each table the fare for that meal. It may be an actual blackboard mounted on the wall or an easel that is moved to each table as needed, or it may be another surface such as a smooth white board, on which the dishes and prices are written in grease pencil or marker.

The main advantage of a blackboard menu is that it can be changed easily. Thus your menu can alter substantially each day, taking advantage of market specials. Deleting items from the menu is also easy, so when you run out of a particular dish, you can simply erase it. Such menus can be quite attractive when carefully written by someone with graphic sense and pleasing handwriting. You can highlight items with different-colored chalk or markers.

The blackboard menu has a couple of drawbacks to keep

in mind. Placement of the menu is tricky. Unless you have a very small restaurant, you will need more than one menu and each of them will need to be located so that all the diners in that area can see it easily. One of my favorite neighborhood restaurants in suburban Virginia has less-than-perfect placement, the board being set so that at certain tables (where, it seems, I'm invariably seated) you have to get up and walk around an iron column to see the blackboard.

Some restaurants avoid the problem of fixing the menu in one (sometimes inconvenient) place by moving the blackboard to each table as customers are seated. This makes seeing the menu much easier, but it can be awkward when other traffic is impeded, or when it comes time to move the board to another table.

Designing the Menu to Sell

The look of your menu is very important. A good graphic design can steer customers to dishes that you particularly want to feature. For instance, the Russian Tea Room, an enormously popular and chic restaurant in New York, recently made a change on their menu, known for its Russian specialties such as blinis, caviar, salmon, and borscht. In the appetizers section of the menu, space was inserted between the zakuska (a selection of Russian appetizers) and the rest of the appetizers. As a result, sales of zakuska increased 15 percent.

The best way to get a good graphic design is to hire a skilled graphic designer. If possible, hire someone who has experience with menus. Explain what you want and how you want it in order to give the designer a clear idea of your needs and wishes.

Work with the designer as much as possible, without getting in his or her way, to communicate your needs. These include: your ideas about the style of menu you envision, the style of the restaurant, the kind of food, and the price range. Set a budget not only for the services of the designer, but for the printing as well. Your designer will be able to advise you on kinds of paper, printing, and suppliers of services. Make sure that the end result fits the image of the restaurant, is pleasing to you, easy to read, and highlights the dishes you most want to sell.

In most cases you will probably want a designer to create a master menu, one on which dishes can be changed without altering the basic design. This will save you having to redesign the menu every time you make a change. Make sure that you let the designer know in advance that you want to be able to make substitutions.

How do you know what you want in a menu? While doing your research, try to gather menus from restaurants that you particularly enjoy or whose menus you especially liked. Many places will give you one. You can use these as the basis for setting up your own. Analyze what you like about individual menus, or what could be done better, given your experience of the restaurant. Perhaps you like the style of type, layout, paper, colors, artwork, the description of dishes—or perhaps you don't.

You might want to feature a particular piece of artwork, perhaps a drawing of the restaurant or a design element indicative of the restaurant. For instance, if you plan to open a fish restaurant, you might want to show a few fish on the menu. Hail Columbia, in Chatham, New York, has a menu that features line drawings by a local artist of scenes around town. Alternatively, you may wish to stick to a very simple card, relying on the type and placement of elements as your main design element.

Having analyzed some menus, you will probably find yourself aware of certain basic design considerations. Whether typewritten, typeset, or hand-lettered, the words on the menu need to be easy to read. This generally means that the type should be of medium size, set in the range of twelve to sixteen points in printer's parlance. The type or lettering style should also be easy to read. Generally speaking, the eye finds upper- and lower-case letters easier to read than all upper case.

Main items should be in larger or bolder type or lettering, and the prices should be placed near enough to the dish that they are easy to read and compare. Check spellings, grammar, and punctuation before you submit material to the designer and again before submitting it to a printer.

The heart of your menu is, of course, the dishes served.

Describe the food appetizingly but honestly. Descriptions should include the method of preparation and the ingredients used, including any particular herbs, spices, and condiments that make the dish stand out. In general, it's a good idea to use adjectives sparingly, letting the food speak for itself and the diners make up their own minds.

If you feature a dish with a standard name such as beouf bourguignon, you should describe it briefly so that diners not familiar with the dish will be attracted to it. Such a description could read: "Chunks of beef stewed with fresh mushrooms, carrots, onions, and burgundy wine." The ingredients are appetizing, and so is the dish. Perhaps the signature of your dish is wild mushrooms. You might then feature that by saying: "Chunks of beef, stewed with winter vegetables, burgundy wine, and finished with wild mushrooms."

When describing dishes, try to avoid florid descriptions that divert attention from the food itself. For instance, it can be irritating for the menu to tell patrons what they should or should not like. An example might be: "The Supreme Delight: Our A-1 super duper deluxe hamburger, with everything, including our ultrasecret dressing—don't miss it!" The description tells me little about it. How is it prepared, what is "everything," what is the "secret" dressing, what's so special?

If you have a strong theme, you may want to capitalize on it in the names of your dishes. If you plan to specialize in a single category of food, you might devise clever names for each of the variations. Be careful, however, of becoming too cute. Not every single item on the menu needs a clever name. It can be overpowering, and can serve to turn people off or confuse them.

Sometimes waiters are encouraged to push certain dishes over others—sometimes contests with prizes are used as incentives for, say, the most individual glasses of wine sold in a week. This must be handled carefully. If patrons feel that they are being pushed toward one dish or another without respect for their requests and wishes, they may feel irritated. Your staff can suggest something, and steer people when they seem to need some help, but they should never pressure customers.

Devising a Wine List

For many restaurants, the wine list is an important part of the menu. When the quality of the wines is commensurate with the quality of the food, the two balance and complement one another. The wine list is also an extra source of profit, particularly welcome in these days of reduced consumption of alcoholic cocktails.

Devising the wine list takes some skill, even if you have a good body of experience. If the wine is too expensive for the menu, patrons will be put off. If it's too mundane, you won't have anything to entice the wine fanciers.

If your menu features primarily American food, you probably won't want to rely too heavily on imports. If your food tends to be light, your wine menu should be suited to the style of food. All of this is plain common sense, but how do you go about finding the right wines from among the thousands that exist?

If you know a lot about wines, great, you probably have an idea of the varieties and even vintages you want to serve. Yet many people don't know the best values for the restaurant market, so if you can, educate yourself as much as possible in advance. Take a wine course, subscribe to wine magazines and newsletters, read and keep at hand several wine reference books, go to wine tastings.

Talk to a good wine merchant or two. Finding a good wine merchant can be invaluable, particularly one that services restaurants. You may want to talk to several to find one with whom you feel comfortable, and one who seems to understand what you are trying to do in creating your restaurant.

You will probably be dealing with five basic categories of wines. These include: the aperitifs, red and white table wines, dessert wines, and sparkling wines.

Aperitifs include sherry, vermouth, and other sweetened wines such as Lillet and are drunk before the meal as a cocktail. Sherry and vermouth come in varying degrees of dryness. Most appetizer wines are fortified, so that the alcoholic content is 15

to 20 percent. This means that they come under certain restrictions in some states.

Table wines are usually served with the meal, although
people increasingly order them before the meal as an aperitif.
Both come in a variety of styles, some light and others heavy,
some dry, others sweet. In general, red wines are heartier than
whites, and few are sweet. White wines can be dry or sweet
and tend to be lighter than reds. Good red and white wines
come from all over the world, particularly North America (most
notably the West Coast, both in variety of styles and quantities), France, Italy, and Spain. Germany produces some of the
finest white wines in a distinctive style that tends to be smooth
and somewhat sweet.

Dessert wines, as the name implies, are served with or
after dessert. They are sweet and include Madeira and port
(primarily from Portugal), sweet sherries (primarily from
Spain), and sauternes (the best are from France).

Sparkling wines such as champagne, Asti Spumante, and
sparkling burgundy are served as aperitifs, with the meal, and
after. Some are sweet, others dry, which makes them quite
versatile.

When you first open, it's a good idea to start with a modest
list, to which you can add as your clientele, as well as your
available capital, grows.

A basic wine list will include wines of each of the basic
categories. You will probably want to stock several house wines
that you can serve by the glass or carafe instead of by the
bottle. These wines usually come bottled in quantity and for
the patron are an economical alternative to an individual bottle. You will need a house red and white, and perhaps a rosé
or blush wine. House wines vary greatly in quality, but the
one thing they should have in common is that they generally
appeal. That means that they need to be middle-of-the-road
wines: not too heavy, not too dry, not too sweet. American wine
tastes are such that today you will probably do well to err on
the side of rather dry house wines, which go well with food.

Finding a good house wine at a moderate price can be a
little tricky to achieve, but there are few things more unpleas-

ant than ordering just a glass of wine when you don't want a whole bottle and finding that it is so inferior to the quality of the food that it damages the whole experience. The better the quality of the house wines, the more of them you will sell, because the better they will taste.

The rest of your wine list should offer a range of better-quality wines. The price list should reflect the range so that even when people are not interested in doubling the cost of their meal with a bottle of fine wine, they can have a decent one that will complement the food. You should include red, white, rosé or blush wines, sparkling, and dessert wines. They should be in vintner-labeled bottles that denote the grape variety or style. Often the year the wine was made, known as the vintage, is listed on the bottle as well.

American wines differ from European and European-style wines in one particularly significant way. Varieties of American wines are almost always known by the kind of grape that is used. European-style wines are known by traditional names related to the area in which they are made. For instance, the equivalent of the classic French red known as Bordeaux is called a cabernet sauvignon in America, after the grape. There are a number of kinds of Bordeaux wines (including white wines), and not all are made strictly with cabernet sauvignon grapes.

Armed with a very basic list of wines, contact several wine distributors in your area. Set up interviews and ask them to bring samples for you to taste. Dealers are often happy to set up tastings. When a dealer arrives, you will want to listen with a few things in mind.

Beware the salesperson who tries to push a particular wine with the incentive, "You'll make a lot of money on this one." The purpose is to have good wines at fair prices, not to make money on your customers with inferior goods. You wouldn't do that with your food, why fall down with your wine?

If you can, you will want to choose a salesperson who has a good knowledge of wine and an understanding of fair pricing. Look for someone who takes pride in the products but also seems to understand your needs and priorities. You need not buy all of your wines from the same purveyor. One might have just the West Coast wines you like, or limit your list to European or Italian or French wines.

Before you buy in quantity, you may want to set up some in-house tastings with food. Only when you serve wines with your food will you really know what you want to stock regularly. You need not have every dish on the menu tested with wine, but you should certainly try your signature dishes and those that are most likely to be popular and ordered with wine.

Dealing With Food Purveyors

You may have a fabulous menu devised with the wonderful recipes you've gathered, but the success of your food will depend largely on the supplies you are able to get.

Reliable wholesale suppliers will play a key role in your success, since in all likelihood they will provide everything including meats, poultry, seafood, fresh produce, dairy products, beverages, baked goods, grocery items, and staples. It pays to shop around and find the purveyors with not only the finest goods but the best service as well. The goods, and their prompt delivery, will be your lifeblood.

So, how do you go about selecting suppliers? As with most things, begin with research. You might talk with other restaurateurs in your area. Talk to the owners or managers and ask who supplies them and other restaurants in the area. If possible, talk to people from several restaurants you like in order to get a range and make up a list of suppliers. The restaurants can even be a little out of your area, as a supplier's range of delivery may be broader than you might think.

Whenever you speak with someone in the business, ask which suppliers they particularly like and why. Ask for the names of sales representatives, making special note of those who come highly recommended.

Once you've got a list of purveyors, start calling them. Identify yourself and explain the nature of your menu, and see about setting up appointments to meet with sales representatives so you can examine their goods and discuss business opportunities. You should be aware that the sales representative, with whom you will be dealing most directly, is in the business of servicing and bringing in new customers. He or she is not usually responsible for the nitty-gritty of credit and payment. For this reason, you may need to speak with the credit manager before you go any further, to determine the company's policy regarding new business.

Being a new business, you may be automatically classified as a bad credit risk for a wholesale supplier. Don't be surprised if the companies you opt to deal with require payment on delivery of the first order or a period of a few weeks or months. Once you've demonstrated that you can and will pay promptly, you may well be extended credit for up to thirty days from the date of delivery.

Service and Price

When you interview suppliers, your choice of one or another should be made with three things in mind: quality should be your first priority, of course, but service and price are not far behind. You cannot make buying decisions without considering all three factors.

Ideally, you want the best-quality goods, delivered frequently and conveniently, at a good price. Far too often people put price ahead of all other considerations when negotiating, but try to keep a balance of the elements in mind.

The one thing you should not compromise on is quality. This does not mean you need to have standing orders for Shiitake mushrooms or the very finest extra virgin olive oil. It does mean that if you accept inferior goods, your food will suffer or your labor costs will soar as you try to make up for the deficiencies. In either case you lose. As in most things, you get what you pay for.

Evaluating the best buy. You may well find that several of the suppliers you interview carry what seem to be the same goods, but at widely varying prices. Check to make sure that the goods are indeed commensurate.

Compare net weights of canned goods; but after purchase you'll also have to be sure that the yields are the same. For instance, a can of tomatoes from one supplier may be listed as thirty-two ounces, just like another's product, but it may cost significantly more—maybe as much as 5 to 7 percent more. You may wonder why, but don't just shrug and order the cheaper one. Find out the reason.

It may be that the cheaper version is featured as a loss leader, or the expensive can is just overpriced, but check to make sure that the yield per can is the same. Some brands have as much as 20 percent more water in the can, and thus fewer tomatoes than the higher-priced one. Obviously, the higher-priced can would be significantly cheaper. A good salesperson will be happy to show you the comparison in your kitchen.

When it comes to items like seafood, produce, meats, and poultry, you have to consider the importance of frequent deliveries. This is particularly true if you intend to serve only the freshest of foods. And these days, with the public becoming ever more aware of the appeal of fresh foods, especially produce, you probably will. In any case, perishable foods such as fresh fish and produce will need to be delivered two or three times a week. If one supplier can't supply you frequently enough, go to another. You may find yourself using more than one to get the goods you need when you need them.

The Importance of Service

In your investigations, you may find that some of the suppliers you interview charge higher prices for just about everything. Oh, the salesperson talks a good line, they deliver frequently, and the other restaurants in the area recommend them, but is it really worth the extra cost? you wonder. If the supplier provides high-quality goods reliably, it probably is.

Maybe you've interviewed another company that seems to have nice goods and at a significantly lower price. You haven't been able to come up with many recommendations, but if they can save you a few hard-earned dollars, maybe they'll be just as or almost as good, you think. Before automatically contracting with the cheaper distributor, ask some questions.

Try to determine how much inventory they keep, how long an order takes, how long they require to fill back orders, and how reliable their deliveries are. The last thing you can afford are deliveries from which items are frequently missing because they are out of stock.

Determine the distributor's payment terms. If you want to give them a chance, see about starting out ordering some of their particularly attractive items and see how they do. If you find you like their goods and their service, you can consider moving more of your business to them.

Tips on Dealing With Sales Representatives

Your working relationship with the sales staff of the various suppliers is crucial to the smooth running of your restaurant. You need to be able to rely on good-quality goods reaching you on schedule, at the agreed-upon price.

One hopes that the salespeople you deal with will all be straightforward and have your best interests in mind when they visit. After all, a good salesperson realizes that good service begets good customers and that in the restaurant business, it isn't today's order that reaps profits but repeat orders for years to come. However, in the event that you find yourself faced with a less-than-sterling character, out to make a few extra bucks on your naïveté, here are a few words of wisdom.

You will probably find that you have become a most popular person among sales representatives in the months before your restaurant opens. Everybody seems to want your business (or as much of it as possible), and they all seem to offer attractive deals of one sort or another. Most sales reps have to meet their quotas, so don't be surprised if you find yourself being pressured to place a large minimum order before you can get the rep to agree to supply the main thing you want.

Unscrupulous suppliers may offer incentives, such as a

very attractive price on an expensive item. A favorite trick is then to substitute a similar but different item on delivery. Unless you are careful, you may find yourself charged for the item you ordered, and not always at the attractive low price that caused you to order it in the first place.

A sales representative may also figure that once you are doing business with his or her company, it will be too much effort to change, and will thus try to take advantage of you. This can take the form of sending you goods you had not ordered, quantities greater than you asked for, or inferior goods. Some sales reps will try to sell you items (food or gadgets), often their own brands, that you do not need and that can run up the bills considerably. Order what you planned to order and try not to be swayed by the persuasive salesperson. You must show that you are in charge and paying attention, that you will brook no nonsense.

Staying on top of things just begins with the initial sales, but once you are up and running, you will also have to keep a watchful eye on deliveries and billings. Goods must be delivered consistently to standard, on time, and at the agreed-upon price.

Make sure that every order is examined upon delivery and that the shipping order (and therefore the resultant invoice) reflects what actually gets unloaded from the truck. Refuse an order if it does not meet your expectations. This is one way to make suppliers understand that you are a serious business person. Mistakes do happen, of course, and a reputable dealer will exchange goods or adjust your invoice without complaint when needed.

Produce. Serving fresh produce is essential in a good restaurant. Indeed, it has become almost mandatory in almost every kind of restaurant from fast-food outlets on up. People these days need not and will not accept frozen or canned vegetables and fruits. High-quality produce in an astonishing variety is available year round at competitive prices. You don't have to serve Chilean raspberries in midwinter if the price seems too high, but you have the option and can probably do it profitably.

Whatever your produce requirements, you will need a reliable produce supplier. These days, they are fairly easy to find. You may have to pay high prices to begin with, but as you go along the more you can show that you are becoming a steady customer, with increasing produce needs, the better the prices are likely to become.

When dealing with produce suppliers, you should be aware that in the beginning they will probably send you the very best fruits and vegetables. After a while they may slack off, trying to deliver you substandard goods. This is a common practice, and one that you will need to monitor.

Here, too, always check each item in the order. If, for instance, a crate of lettuce includes heads that are wilted, either refuse delivery (if you can afford to be without the acceptable heads that day) or demand credit on future deliveries. Keep your standards high; you're paying the same price no matter what.

If you live in an area that has local seasonal specialties, don't be afraid to take advantage of local suppliers for those special items. It may be tempting to switch to a local farmer for all of your produce in the summer when, say, the corn, beans, lettuce, and berries are local. But be careful. If you stop using your regular supplier entirely during the local season, you may have a difficult time resuming your business relationship come winter. Better to take advantage of a few special things locally and leave the basics to your usual purveyor.

Meat, Poultry, and Seafood

Purveyors of meat, poultry, and seafood can provide all kinds of wonderful goods these days. It's not uncommon for seafood suppliers to drive from Maine several times a week to deliver fresh lobsters to destinations hundreds of miles away. The variety of goods and often their quality is increasing, as the American restaurant-going public demands the best in food.

For an increasing number of restaurants, however, profit requires volume, and so the nature of some kinds of packaging has changed. You may think the wisest approach to selling beef is to buy full sides and have your chef butcher them. But you may find that your operation cannot afford the time and expertise of such a highly skilled technician and that you will do better to order prepacked cuts.

You will have to decide on the basis of what your menu requires. The per-serving price of whole chickens is much less than precut chicken cutlets, and a skilled cook can bone and fillet a chicken quickly. The bones can also be used to make stock and the extra pieces used in other dishes. But if your menu features quickly cooked fillet dishes, you may be wasting precious time and money in butchering and cooking the less desirable chicken portions. And stock is not free when it's taken a chef three hours to make it. Most foods can be found in convenient portions, whatever you find them to be.

When it comes to seafood, freshness is vital. Seafood spoils quickly, and so the fresher it arrives to you, the longer you will be able to serve it. Never accept delivery of fish that is old. Fresh fish has a clear not cloudy eye, and the skin is firm not slimy. If it smells fishy, it's old.

Some fish and seafoods are best bought frozen, especially when the items come from a considerable distance, or you cannot rely on a totally seasonal menu. Individually quick-frozen shrimp, scallops, squid, chopped clams, lobster tails, king crab legs, midwestern trout, and catfish all can be successfully frozen with minimal effect on the taste.

You may find that your meat, poultry, and seafood purveyors will need to have it demonstrated to them that, as with your other suppliers, you will accept only what you ordered and only in top-rate condition. Any substandard goods should be refused and any wrong orders should be credited promptly.

Frozen Foods

Discussion of fresh foods brings us to the question of whether to use frozen foods or not. Frozen foods tend to be cheaper, especially those that can be bought in bulk and kept on hand. However, a good rule to follow is never to have too much inventory on hand, since it ties up your money. Frozen foods also have a definite freezer life that is generally not more than a few months.

If you plan to open a restaurant that features budget-priced meals and to operate on high volume, you may be able to use a variety of frozen foods to advantage. Suppliers often carry a wide range of prepared frozen foods. You will need to select carefully, however, to assure good quality at a fair price.

One type of frozen food that makes good sense these days is cryovac-packed meats, poultry, and fish. Unlike traditionally frozen foods, these have been vacuum-sealed before freezing, which helps to maintain the quality of the food. They also come in portions of uniform weight, so that you can control easily the cost of a dish. This results in virtually no waste.

Such foods are particularly useful for single servings such as chops, steaks, cutlets, and fillets. Cryovac-packaged foods tend to be more expensive than large portions requiring butchering preparation, but the waste is minimal and the time and labor savings can be worth it for certain dishes.

QUESTIONS TO ASK YOUR SALES REPRESENTATIVE

1. What is the minimum order? By the case? Dollar amount?
2. What are the credit terms?

3. What is the delivery schedule to the area?
4. What is the lead time for ordering?
5. Will the supplier call in advance of delivery to let me know if ordered items are temporarily out of stock?
6. Have deliveries ever been disrupted as a result of labor disputes?

How to Get Good Service

We've talked above about keeping demanding standards, tracking orders, and standing firm as methods for training your suppliers to give you good service. You must see that they live up to their responsibilities as purveyors, but as a buyer, you have responsibilities as well.

First and foremost, always pay your suppliers as promptly as possible. As one restaurateur told me, "Always pay your suppliers first. Always, always, always." This more than anything will go a long way to assuring you good service.

Second, place your orders as regularly and as much in advance as possible. Occasionally, you will need to make last-minute orders and changes, but try to keep it to a minimum.

Third, try to keep a good rapport with the people who service your account. Being pleasant but firm helps them do their jobs.

Fourth, try to keep the delivery people disposed to your establishment. This last point is important on several counts. For one, they eat out, too, and they probably talk to a lot of people. You want to be spoken of highly in order to build a good reputation. Being good to the delivery people entails being pleasant (both you and your staff), being available when they deliver, and having a pleasant environment for them to deliver their goods. Simple steps like having a designated area for their delivery that is kept open for them or offering the odd soft drink on a hot day and a cup of coffee on a cold one can make your stop one to which the driver looks forward.

With your menu clearly laid out, you can move on to setting up efficient operating systems. If the food is what attracts people to your restaurant, it is efficient service and systems that make them feel properly welcomed and well treated.

CHAPTER

Setting Up Systems

Establishing good control systems from the outset can help make or break your restaurant. The better the systems you have for maintaining proper inventory, portion size, and food handling, and for handling reservations, accounting, and billing, the easier it will be to please your guests. The well-organized restaurant is, in short, a pleasure both to visit *and* to manage.

Inventory

One important system in the efficiently run restaurant is that of inventory control.

You must know on a regular basis what you have in stock, what it is worth, which items are used most frequently, and which tend to remain on the shelves unused for long periods. A good inventory is a useful tool in helping to determine the profitability—or lack thereof—of your restaurant. Frequent inventories are also a good way to discourage pilfering.

An inventory system must be easy to use in order for it to be effective. Create a plan for storing the foods, then prepare your inventory sheets to reflect the organization of the shelving. That way you don't have to hunt from page to page for items.

Some suppliers provide inventory sheets for their goods so that you can easily check off what's needed. This then serves as an order form. If you choose to use these, arrange the shelves accordingly.

All foods should be stored so that they are easy to see. Like items should be stored with one another.

When foods arrive and are stored, they should be checked off on the inventory sheets or in a book and their numbers added to the totals. Prices should be noted either on these sheets or in a separate recording system.

You might also want to break down the prices into cost per serving for the various items. Say, for example, you purchase a box of twenty steaks which costs forty-five dollars. You could have a column on your sheet that states the cost per box, and the serving cost of $2.25. That way, each time you reorder you can see whether the cost has risen. This gives you an instant reading of prices. That way, you will know at a glance when to lay in a supply of a particular item when it goes on sale, and how much you might need. You can also tell whether you need to change the price on your menu to allow for an escalation in the cost of the raw goods.

Keeping the inventory when foods are delivered is one portion of the job. Another is to take note of foods that have been used. This should be done at regular intervals, perhaps weekly or monthly. In either case, at the end of each month an update should be made showing how much of each item is left and what it is worth.

You will also need to list, separately, credits from suppliers due to breakage and spoilage. These figures, known as the closing inventory, are useful for preparing a profit-and-loss statement (see Chapter 5).

Another purpose of keeping a close inventory is to determine possible areas of waste. When you first start a restaurant, there is bound to be food wastage as the restaurant's patterns of usage develop. By knowing just what you have on hand and what you need, you can more easily keep from overstocking certain items and understocking (which can cause shortages) others. You will also have to determine from experience how quickly your suppliers can deliver the items you need. (For more about suppliers, see Chapter 8.)

Methods of Billing

One of the systems you will have to set up in your restaurant is the method for billing. The restaurant business is known as a cash-rich business, in part because so many people pay their bills with it. The higher the average bill in your restaurant is, however, the more likely you are to need to be able to accept checks (also considered cash) and credit-card payments. Some restaurants will extend credit to favored customers and bill them on a monthly basis, but this is becoming less common.

The easiest form of payment, as far as accounting is concerned, is cash. Customers hand over the greenbacks (or a check, as from an accounting standpoint the two are interchangeable). The payment then enters the cash register and the amount is recorded in a sales journal at the end of the day. The money is then deposited in the bank.

However, before the deposit is made, the books must be reconciled. This means that the guest checks are compared against the amounts received. In the best of all possible worlds there would never be mistakes, but this simply is not the case. Now and again someone will be overcharged and another undercharged. Credit-card charges must be reconciled, too.

One of the problems with handling lots of cash is the way it can disappear. It's so easy to take a few bills from the register, particularly since sometimes you have to draw from the cash drawer for petty-cash purchases. For more information on cash control systems, see page 149.

And yes, light-fingered employees do exist, making cash control systems all the more important.

Credit-card charges. These days it seems virtually impossible to run a full-service restaurant without taking credit cards. You needn't worry about taking them if you run a pizza parlor, lunch counter, or takeout restaurant, but if you run a full-service dinner restaurant, you will be faced with this apparent necessity.

The larger the check, the more frequently diners wish to use credit cards. Indeed, not many people like going around with large chunks of cash in their wallets these days, and when people are eating out on an expense account, a credit card is by far the easiest method of keeping track of their bills.

Taking credit cards is thus almost a given, although some restaurants have begun refusing them. There are advantages and disadvantages to taking them. Let's look at the disadvantages first.

The bookkeeping involved in taking credit cards is more complicated than that for cash. You have to apply to the company for reimbursement, which, depending on the company, can take up to several weeks. The wait can be especially hard on a fledgling business. Doing business with credit-card companies is also not free. You will be charged 4 to 5 percent of receipts. This added cost will need to be reflected in your menu.

The advantages of taking credit cards are important, too. For one, they guarantee payment. If you take a bad check, you are likely to be out the money, where a credit-card company will make good. The majority of people in our credit-card society have credit cards and like to use them. If they see that you don't carry at least one of the most popular cards, they may well not eat in your restaurant. People also sometimes order a little more liberally, knowing that what they buy can be paid for at a later time.

One way to keep your prices low and still use credit cards is to have a separate price. A bar-restaurant called 20 Railroad Street in Great Barrington, Massachusetts, for instance, has a notice printed at the top of its menu stating that they accept credit cards, but using one will add 5 percent to the cost of the meal. This is a very fair method, since those who wish to pay cash can save a little money, and those who wish to pay with a credit card can do so.

A note about handling gratuities on credit cards: even if most checks are paid with credit cards, payment of tips to employees is usually done in cash, taken from the register as petty cash.

Check systems. Unless you are a very small operation and can oversee the work of every person on the waiting staff, you will probably want to investigate some sort of system for balancing the amount of money taken in with the amount of food and beverages dispensed. Mistakes are bound to happen, and the more you can safeguard against them, the better. Also, sad as it is to report, you may on occasion find yourself with an unscrupulous employee who manages to keep a certain amount of money that should go into the register.

You might want to investigate buying a computer system for your restaurant. Such systems cut down enormously on the amount of paperwork and figuring that each person on the waiting staff must do. The usual procedure is, upon taking an order, to enter it on the computer; the order is almost simultaneously received in the kitchen and at the bar. Prices are automatically assigned to the items and then totaled by the computer.

With such systems, it is difficult to serve a lobster dinner but charge for a hamburger, since it's been entered in several places, including the kitchen where the food is produced.

Another method for keeping track is to use a precheck system. Under this method, the order is taken and the items rung on a register. The register produces two copies of the items. The second, or duplicate, is then the one that is used to alert the kitchen or bar staff of an order. Only the dupes can be used to place an order. During the course of the meal, someone (you, the host or hostess, or senior waiting person) is then responsible for correcting any mistakes made.

At the end of the meal the dupe slips are collected and placed with the cash. If needed, they can be used to run a further check. The machine will have kept a copy of all transactions, which can then be balanced by the bookkeeper.

Reservations

Depending on the size and style of your restaurant, you may want to consider taking reservations. Some people feel that it is imperative to take them in order to be sure to fill seats. The thought is that people will not travel and wait if they cannot get a table and that everyone will want a table at the same time. Other successful restaurateurs feel that by not taking reservations, they can ensure a more even turnover by seating people as they arrive.

Terry Moore, of the Old Mill in South Egremont, Massachusetts, feels that by not taking reservations for parties under six, his tables turn up to half again as often. Which translates to up to 50 percent more patrons served.

The approach at the Old Mill is to open at five and serve until ten. Moore finds that the early birds come between five and five-thirty. That means they are finished by about seven. If he were to take a reservation for seven-thirty, the table couldn't be used for half an hour, but if he has someone waiting in the bar, they can be seated right away. The table will again be free again at about nine-thirty, time for a last seating before the end of the evening.

At his restaurant people come constantly between five and nine-thirty. They have also set it up so that you feel welcome from the moment you step inside the restaurant. Another part of the overall strategy has been to make the bar as pleasant and as cozy a place to wait as possible.

If you choose to take reservations, be sure to have a system. One person should handle reservations in order that mistakes and duplications are not made. This person should also handle the seating plan, slotting in parties for particular tables. Adjustments can be made at the time of arrival, if needed, but an overall plan should be known.

Reservations can be staggered or at set intervals. Most people find that staggering reservations makes it easier on the kitchen and waiting staff, as the flow of courses is kept constant and there is less of a backlog in the kitchen and in the dining room. Others find that it's easier to have set times, and the kitchen can gear up to prepare a large number of meals at one time.

When making reservations, you must keep in mind the amount of time each party will take. In general, for a full-service dinner restaurant you can figure parties of two will take about an hour and a half, parties of three or four about two hours, and larger parties two and a half hours. This will help determine the number of turns you can expect from each table on a busy night and thus how many people you can book. There's another general rule you might find helpful to keep in mind when thinking about reservations: people tend to eat later on weekends than on weeknights.

You will need to set a policy on how long to hold reservations. If people are a few minutes late, the table should be held. More than that, though, and the table should be given to someone else, perhaps a walk-in who has been waiting. You might consider giving extra leeway to large parties who have a more difficult time organizing. Unlike small parties, who may well not show if they are more than ten or fifteen minutes late, larger parties usually do. You are also less likely to have a large party waiting to fill that space.

Sanitation and Food Handling

The importance of good systems for sanitation and handling of food cannot be stressed enough. It is vital to your reputation and the success of your restaurant that the cleanliness of the premises, the food, and the employees always remains beyond reproach.

This is not an easy task, given the nature of the business, in that restaurants have a large volume of traffic, produce a great quantity of food, and have many employees. Still, you must at all times be aware of the importance of cleanliness, for to be lax or unaware can lead to serious consequences.

Begin with your staff. People are the main means of transmitting bacteria and viruses that cause disease. The more you can reduce the risks of possible transmission of such organisms, the less likely you are to have sick customers or staff.

In this area you will have to be firm, if not downright strict, in keeping your employees up to acceptable standards. Begin by educating them. It's not enough to set rules and expect people to live by them. In order for the rules to work, your employees must understand that it's for the welfare of the customers, and of themselves as well.

Some of your workers may have lax attitudes toward cleanliness. Those not originally from our culture may have different notions of cleanliness. If there is a language barrier, you may also have to try harder and more frequently to educate them as to the rules.

Try your best to get through to all people who handle food and utensils the importance of sanitation. It's not merely a matter of passing the health inspections that your town might require, it's for the good of the restaurant and everyone you serve.

SANITATION RULES FOR EMPLOYEES

The following is a list of the most common rules that must be followed by those handling food, both kitchen staff and waiting staff:

1. Employees must be healthy so they don't pass along infectious diseases to fellow workers and customers.
2. Hands must be clean in order to work with food. They must be washed with soap after every visit to the rest room in order to keep from spreading food-borne diseases.
3. Employees must not sneeze over food. It spreads infectious organisms. If employees sneeze and cover their mouths with a hand, the hands must be washed.
4. Food should never be tasted with the fingers or with

a spoon that is then put back in the pot. A small portion should be put on a plate and tasted with a separate utensil. The tasted food should never be returned to the pot.

5. Employees must be clean. They must not smell. Fingernails must be kept short and clean. Hair must be kept short or tied back. Some municipalities and states require that kitchen workers wear hats or hair nets to keep hair from dropping into food. There are few things less appetizing than finding foreign hairs in one's food.

6. Glasses and cutlery should be handled only by the bases and handles.

7. Food cannot be served or mixed by hand. Utensils must be used.

8. Smoking should not be allowed near food preparation.

9. Employees must wear only clean clothing and uniforms. Hands must be wiped on towels, not aprons. Aprons should be changed when they become soiled.

In addition to personal habits and systems, employees must get in the habit of cleaning as they go. Not only does it make the restaurant more sanitary, but clean surfaces make food preparation tasks easier to perform.

Surfaces must be washed in hot water with soap, particularly those that have been used to prepare meats, poultry, and fish. Utensils that have been used for such preparation must be washed in hot, soapy water before being used again.

Handling food. The proper handling of food, from the moment it enters the kitchen to the plating of each dish just prior to serving, is important for safety. As mentioned above, meats, poultry, and fish must be handled with special care, as they can easily become breeding grounds for harmful bacteria.

All food should be handled carefully, to be sure that it is of the highest quality. This process starts with delivery. Check everything as it arrives. In fact, don't accept delivery of items until they have been deemed to be of the quality you ordered. It's awfully easy to overlook a box of lettuce when ten crates of fruits and vegetables come in. But if half of the heads have begun to deteriorate, you've just bought very expensive lettuce.

When deliveries are made, all fresh foods must be taken care of immediately. Frozen foods cannot be allowed to defrost. If frozen foods arrive defrosted, refuse delivery. You cannot refreeze them successfully without deterioration of quality and in some cases spoilage.

Refrigerate poultry, raw meats, and shellfish immediately upon delivery. Do not store any foods near pot-washing areas, where they may be contaminated with detergents or waste water, or on the floor, where they may be sprayed with pesticides.

Proper treatment of food during preparation is the next step in keeping your restaurant safe. Frozen food should be defrosted in the refrigerator or in cold water and used promptly. Defrosted food can deteriorate rapidly. If you must defrost food in a warm kitchen, make sure the food is wrapped tightly in plastic.

Food should be cooked to at least 140 degrees Fahrenheit in order to kill potential harmful bacteria. Increasingly, eggs have been found to be a source of salmonella poisoning. This means that you should not use raw eggs in sauces or other food preparations. Most sauces and desserts requiring raw eggs can be altered to use slowly cooked eggs. Leftovers must be reheated to 140 degrees Fahrenheit to kill the bacteria that tend to grow rapidly in them.

Food that is to be kept and not served immediately should be cooled quickly to forty-five degrees Fahrenheit or below after cooking. To cool rapidly, spread hot cooked foods in a pan in a shallow layer and cover before putting in the refrigerator.

Storage. All fresh foods, whether cooked or not, should be stored refrigerated at forty-five degrees Fahrenheit or lower to maintain quality. Frozen foods should be stored at zero degrees Fahrenheit. All boxes and crates should be cleaned, if necessary, before being stored in a refrigerator or freezer. Packages should be sealed tightly.

Refrigerators and freezers should be cleaned inside and

out periodically. Spills should be wiped up when made in order to minimize later cleanup and safety hazards.

Nonrefrigerated foods should be stored in a clean, ventilated area off the floor. Foods should not be placed near damp walls, pipes, or drain openings. Storeroom floors should be of a material that can be easily cleaned. Spills should be wiped up immediately.

Stored food should be rotated. One easy way to do this is to place the newest shipments of foods behind those already on hand.

Check boxes and bags on arrival for cockroaches and other bugs. A single box that arrives with a few cockroaches can infest an entire restaurant.

Dishwashing. One potential source of food contamination is improperly washed dishes. All items used for handling food, from plates, glassware, utensils, pots, and pans, must be washed well in hot soapy water. Staff must be trained in the importance of a thorough cleaning of each item.

You will need adequate facilities to clean dishes properly. Many municipalities require separate sinks for pots and dishes. (Note also that food should never be prepared in a sink that is used for dishwashing.) Don't skimp on hot water, even though it can be expensive. All dishes, glassware, utensils, and pots and pans should be rinsed in 170-degree-Fahrenheit water unless a sanitizing agent is used. If one is, the water temperature can be as low as 140 degrees Fahrenheit.

And don't skimp on detergent or other supplies. Scrubbing brushes should be provided for thorough cleaning of pots and pans.

Portion Control

An important element of cost management is the size of the portions you serve. By determining the most appealing and efficient sizes of portions, you can set up guidelines your cooks and bartenders easily can follow.

Such determinations must be based on a combination of factors, including the cost of foods as well as the psychological aspects of expected size and perceived value. If your restaurant is to be a steak-and-potatoes kind of place located in an area where the size of portions determines the value of a restaurant in the public mind, you will probably want to fit into the local customs and serve large portions. You may need to charge more or limit the menu substantially in order to meet the perceived-portion need.

Aesthetics also plays a major role in determining portion size. Too large a portion of a particular dish overwhelms everything else and can look unappetizing. Too small a portion looks stingy. Another factor to consider when determining what makes a portion look large or small is the other elements to be served on the plate.

Once you've decided on the optimum portion size, cost out the dish. If the selling price comes out too high, you might consider making the portion a little smaller and possibly adding an inexpensive item to the plate. If you cannot find an acceptable alternative, don't serve the item, unless you consider it vital to the success of the restaurant.

Many restaurant suppliers provide already portioned foods such as meats, poultry, and fish. In general, this is likely to be a fairly expensive way to go on a per-pound basis, but it does guarantee little wastage and consistent portion sizes. In addition, you save on the expensive staff time needed to butcher or otherwise prepare the ingredients for cooking.

Some restaurants weigh portions. If you choose this method, make it part of the advance preparation, so time isn't wasted during a rush. If you choose this method, don't let customers see it. There are few things as frustrating as standing in line at the Dairy Queen for ten minutes, ordering a soft-serve cone, watching it being prepared, weighed, and then seeing it thrown away because it didn't come in at quite the right weight.

Some restaurants have begun to rely on preportioned, pre-prepared, precooked entrées. This is an expensive alternative. It may allow you to expand the menu a bit, but the price will be high, and the quality something over which you have no control.

Once you and your chef have decided on portion sizes, you

will have to educate your staff. State clearly the quantities on any master recipes you use. Instruct each person who handles food about the portions they are to use. This includes prep people, cooks and chefs, and even serving people, who may be called on to serve salad and dessert. This makes up part of staff training, and may not be needed until you are almost ready to open.

Record Keeping

Good accounting and record-keeping procedures are vitally important to a well-run business. Only by knowing how much money comes in, how much goes out, and how it is used along the way can you assess the profitability of your restaurant.

For the first year or two, you probably can't expect to show a profit. You will be building the business and probably paying for your renovations and start-up costs. It's all too easy to find yourself caught up in merely staying afloat and not keep good records.

If you have a good system of keeping records in place from the beginning, it will be far easier down the road to assess your needs and profitability. You will be in a better position to make changes, should the need arise. You will know if money is being siphoned off. If you find yourself in the enviable position of being successful, you will also know it and be able to concentrate on the business of serving your clientele.

How to start? Begin by creating a daily-expenditure-and-sales journal. Such a journal, which your accountant can help tailor to your needs, should list all money that goes out and comes in. This information is then translated to a ledger sheet, which tracks all the monies for a given period, usually a month. You may choose to create a ledger sheet for each area, including payroll, purchases, and sales.

Next, using the information from your ledgers, set up a profit-and-loss statement like the one discussed in Chapter 5. This time, instead of projected costs and revenues, you will use real ones. The profit-and-loss statement is a useful tool for telling you how your business is progressing. This should be made up on a regular basis, monthly or quarterly, by you or your accountant.

Your ledger sheets are also useful for creating a balance sheet that tells you how much your business is worth at any particular time. A balance sheet takes your current assets from the ledgers—including cash on hand and in the bank, value of your inventory, any prepaid taxes or insurance premiums, and your fixed assets, including the value of the real estate, furnishings, and equipment—and balances them against your liabilities. Liabilities include any outstanding bills as well as short- and long-term loans.

Good systems that have been thought out in advance, that have been adjusted to suit the practical day-to-day operations of your restaurant, require a daily investment of time and consideration. But over time they will prove of value to you in managing your business to success.

CHAPTER

10

Equipping
and Furnishing
Your Restaurant

Once you have a handle on the basic design of your restaurant, it's time to think about equipping and furnishing it.

In some cases equipping and designing the restaurant go hand in hand, particularly in the case of the kitchen plan, or when you have an architect/designer who plans everything and whose furnishings are vital to the design. More often, however, people find that once they have a very basic understanding of how the spaces will work, they then begin the planning process of outfitting it.

As with most things, the more you can plan in advance of the actual moment you buy a furnishing or piece of equipment, the better off you will be. You will know more exactly what it is you need, and will thus lessen your risks of buying too much or too little equipment. By waiting and surveying the marketplace carefully, you may also be able to take advantage of any sales or other cost-saving advantages.

Equipping the Kitchen

Once you know the logical places for the various functional areas of your kitchen (work stations, storage, preparation, dishwashing; see Chapter 7) you can begin thinking of the actual placement of appliances and equipment.

First you need to know just what equipment you will need. There again, we're back to the kind of menu and number of people you'll be serving. It's best to consider your needs from start to finish. You'll need shelves and storage area, even if you only serve steamers and lobster straight from the boats. You know that you will require surfaces on which to prepare food. Refrigeration is a must, and probably a certain amount of freezer capacity as well. And so on.

Call an equipment dealer or two with a list of the equipment you'll need. Even if you don't end up buying from these particular dealers, you will at least know the dimensions and availability of equipment.

Learn the specifications on each of the elements needed so you can think about placement. Most will need electricity and some will require plumbing, so their location may be dictated by available utility lines.

Cooking Surfaces

Unless you plan to serve only ice cream and cold-cut sandwiches, you will need cooking surfaces. If your meals are to be varied, you will probably require a range with at least four and up to eight burners (gas, if possible) and at least two ovens. In today's kitchen, a broiler is often one of the most-used pieces of equipment. It's quick and clean.

In addition to a range, oven, and broiler, you will have to have a hood and exhaust system. This can be one of the most expensive pieces of equipment in the kitchen, even though it doesn't seem to do much—except ventilate the kitchen and prevent fires. Local health codes often have strict requirements about the type of system you must use, so check before buying.

Other sorts of ovens are used for special preparations. If you plan to bake your own breads and pastries, you will need bake ovens or convection ovens. You will probably do well to have a microwave oven for quickly heating foods that have been prepared in advance. A stew that was made earlier in the day tastes far better reheated in a microwave than if it's been kept warm for hours in a steam table.

If you plan to do fast food, you may need only a grill or broiler and a deep fryer. You may well not need a deep fryer or a grill unless you plan to make a specialty of fried food and burgers. If you do plan to serve fried food, you should be aware that you will probably have to have extra equipment to deal with the grease, and you may find that your insurance premiums are substantially greater due to the increased fire and safety hazards. Also, since the grease enters the air, it coats everything in a kitchen, which will be reflected in increased cleaning costs.

Preparation Surfaces

No matter what kind of establishment you open, you will need counter space to prepare food. You may need only a few feet of space, or you may need several large stations, depending on the variety of foods you prepare.

Wooden worktables are generally the easiest to work on, particularly when it comes to chopping, when you often have to use a chopping board. Many states, however, do not allow wooden surfaces, since they can trap bacteria. Stainless steel is thus the surface of general choice.

Any worktable should be at least six feet long, if possible, and if it is made of stainless steel, at least fourteen gauge. Chopping boards should be generous in size to allow you to move freely—at least three feet wide and the depth of the table. Many health departments require that chopping boards be made of scratch-resistant plastic.

Worktables should have storage shelves underneath, if

possible. Having your equipment right where it is to be used will save on labor and add to overall efficiency.

Cooling Equipment

Refrigeration is an obvious necessity. If you plan to run a small lunch counter of a few stools or a couple of booths, you may be able to get away with one or two under-counter refrigerators. Just about anything larger, however, and you will need lots of space.

Most restaurants require a walk-in refrigerator as well as a reach-in one. A walk-in refrigerator provides cold storage for those items you keep in bulk for several days at a time. These range in size from about six feet square (about the smallest useful size) to room-size units. Reach-in refrigerators come in a variety of styles and sizes. Upright ones with glass doors are helpful for finding things quickly and easily, but more important, make sure the ones you purchase have a light and thermometer. Counter units, often with drawers, are most useful for quickly and efficiently removing single servings of items directly at the work station.

You will probably need freezer capacity in addition to refrigeration. Again, freezers come in a wide variety of styles and sizes, ranging from room-size walk-in freezers to locker and upright styles not much larger than home versions. If you plan to serve a good deal of ice cream, you may want to investigate ice-cream freezers, which also come in a variety of sizes.

Storage

Every restaurant needs storage space. Your refrigerators and freezer are one sort of storage, of course, but you will need to consider the more mundane forms such as shelving.

You will need shelf storage for staples, frequently used items, kitchenware, dishware and glassware, and linens. Each should be kept in a convenient location. Staples can be stored in a remote part of the kitchen or storage area, where they can be reached easily for restocking but are not taking up precious preparation space. Frequently used food items for each meal need to be near the preparation areas.

Kitchenware must be within reach of the specific preparation areas (sauté pans and cooking utensils, for instance, must be near the stove). Plates must be near or even on the stove (in a warming area or nearby warm shelf) so that food can be plated easily. Dishware must be located for the serving staff to set up tables (this may be in an area near but not in the kitchen). Table linens must be stored where they are accessible to serving staff. They can even be stored in an attractive piece of furniture in the dining room.

You will need a variety of shelving. Stainless-steel shelves within a walk-in refrigerator make very good sense. At the worktables, you will want storage under the table and perhaps on a shelf above. Staples and linens can be stored on wooden shelves. All shelving, however, must be at least six inches (often required by the health code) off the floor to allow for cleaning. This applies to appliances as well.

Buying Equipment

Buy restaurant-grade equipment whenever possible. It can be much more expensive than goods you would buy for home use, but in the case of large appliances in particular, such equipment will prove substantially cheaper in the long run. Small appliances, such as food processors, blenders, and mixers (if you plan to mix in small quantities) can be just sturdy, good-quality machines rather than commercial grade. You can upgrade later, if you need to.

You need not buy all new restaurant equipment, either. Some used equipment is perfectly good and will have years of service left. Equipment dealers often take used equipment in trade when a client decides to upgrade. They also buy at auction when businesses fail.

Most restaurant equipment auctions are open to the public,

and there is no reason why you can't buy at them. They can be a great way to save money, since you cut out paying the middleman. As with all auctions, you will need to follow two rules.

First, thoroughly inspect all the merchandise during the preview. If you cannot tell whether a piece of equipment is in good shape, don't even consider bidding on it. Note the lot number so that you will bid on the exact piece of equipment you're interested in. Second, set a maximum price in your mind before the bidding begins. If the price goes over the price you had planned in advance, drop out. Once the bidding is under way, it's easy to be swept up by auction fever and end up paying far more than you ever intended.

BUYING USED EQUIPMENT

When buying any kind of used equipment, you must be careful to determine its condition and its worth. You will want to find out as much about the condition of the equipment as possible and, in addition, where it was used and how.

The following are a few issues to consider in determining the worth of a particular piece.

- Try to find out the age and general condition of the piece.
- Does it have many working pieces, and if so, how easy will they be to replace?
- Was the piece regularly serviced and generally well cared for?
- Try to discover why the piece you're interested in is being sold.
- Are any warranties still in effect?
- What is the average market price for such a piece used, and new?

- If the piece needs work, how much will it cost to put it in good order?

Buying used equipment is largely a personal matter, whether you go through a dealer or an individual. There are advantages to both. A dealer may have a reputation that needs protecting. If there is a problem, a dealer may thus be in a better position to make amends than an individual, particularly one who has just gone out of business. On the other hand, a dealer will probably have to charge a higher price than a private individual to cover overhead, business costs, and profit.

Certain categories of equipment are better risks buying used than others. Nonmotorized equipment such as tables, counters, sinks, racks, and shelving are safe bets when bought used—a close inspection will usually reveal any problems. Slicers, toasters, and fryers are pretty good risks as well. Ovens should be checked for insulation, thermostat, and warpage to ensure that they will give lasting service.

Refrigeration equipment, including refrigerators, freezers, and ice makers, is best bought new. Refrigerators have complicated mechanisms, which can easily fail. It can be difficult to tell if there is a weak point in the system of a used piece. The cost to your business of replacing a compressor for an older machine can be totally out of proportion to the savings in its purchase price.

Mixers are also risky used investments, unless bought fairly new. Good commercial mixers are very sturdy and last years, but once you begin to have problems, they seem to compound, increasing repair costs dramatically.

When buying any kind of motorized mechanical equipment, you will need to arrange for service. New equipment will come with a warranty, but you may wish to arrange for a service contract as well. These can be expensive, but regular maintenance of equipment is essential to assuring years of usefulness. Even if you buy used equipment, you should be able to arrange for emergency and regular service through a dealer or maintenance company. If you are particularly handy, you may be able to perform some of the regular functions yourself.

You are probably better off letting a service company check your mechanical equipment for the greasing, belt changing, gear oiling, and such that is part of regular service. When it comes to routine and easy-to-reach tasks—such as cleaning filters and refrigerator coils, checking the accuracy of thermostats, cleaning oven, broiler, and burner parts, and replacing door springs—you can save a lot of money and time by doing it in-house (by either you or your employees) on a regular basis.

THE MOST BASIC EQUIPMENT

Regardless of the size of your restaurant or the style of your menu, there are a number of basic pieces of equipment you will need to have. These include:

Cooking surfaces (such as broiler, range and/or grill)
Ovens (conventional and microwave for quick heating)
Hood and exhaust system
Fire-prevention equipment
Refrigeration, walk-in
Refrigeration, reach-in
Freezer
Ice maker
Slicer
Coffeemaker
Worktables
Sinks (separate ones for food preparation, dishwashing, and
    hand washing)
Dishwasher and tables
Shelving for food storage, dry and refrigerated
Shelving or rack for pots and pans

You may need the following appliances, but you should assess those needs to discover how much you would really use them.

Blender
Mixer
Food processor
Steamer
Toaster
French fryer
Soup warmer
Convection oven for baking
Bread warmer
Steam table

In addition, you will need a wide variety of kitchenware such as pots and pans, bowls, cutting boards, scales, knives, spoons, ladles, spatulas, forks, whisks, tongs, thermometers, scrapers, scoops, shakers, brushes, scissors, can opener.

What the Public Sees

The look of each restaurant is different and to a large degree a matter of your personal taste. It's a chance to show off your sense of style in a dining ambience. This is, of course, not true if you run a franchise restaurant, in which everything has been designated by the home office.

Many people know the kind of look they want to achieve almost instantly. Such was the case with Donald Selby of Hail Columbia, who knew the moment he walked into the three-story Victorian brick building with gingerbread porches in Chatham, New York, what the style of the future restaurant would be. He capitalized on the building's architecture by creating an interior reminiscent of the gaslight era.

Bruce Marder goes to great lengths to create fantasies such as DC3 in Santa Monica, California, and the Jules Verne–like interior of his West Beach Café in Venice, California.

On the other end of the spectrum, many successful simple restaurants do practically nothing to please customers with their interiors. Indeed, most of us would be a little put off if certain kinds of joints placed any emphasis on their dining room. How good could a clam shack be if it actually looked like a restaurant? Could the barbecue really be good at a dolled-up barbecue joint?

Then there are those restaurants that can rely on their location to provide the charm. The screened-porch dining room at the Pier Street Restaurant in Oxford, a simple crab restaurant on the Tred Avon River of Maryland's Eastern Shore, provides the best view any diner could want of the scenery of the river. Ducks glide by, diners watch a small ferry carrying cars and customers across the river, sailboats dock at the restaurant. At such a location plastic tablecloths seem the only appropriate option. The same is true at Chauncey Creek in Kittery Point, Maine, where most of the brightly painted picnic tables are located outside on a dock, and the pristine woods and rocks lining the estuary form a panorama.

By far the greater number of restaurants must pay more attention to the furnishings from a practical standpoint, as the elements tend to be more complicated. Your board of health and fire departments may have regulations concerning the front of the house in addition to the kitchen. Areas covered in their jurisdictions include rugs, wall coverings, ceiling material, paint, exposed surfaces, and work stations. Check with your local authorities before fully decorating and furnishing your restaurant.

Furnishings

The furnishings of a dining room, including the tables and chairs, lighting, floor covering, and window treatments, are integral to your restaurant from a functional as well as a decorative standpoint. Finding the right furnishings need not be difficult, but it is important to give it thorough thought and planning.

Tables and chairs. These two furnishings can be the most important as far as the comfort of your customers is concerned. A table that is too small to accommodate the plates needed for a meal or the elbows of an expansive diner can be a problem. An uncomfortable chair can leave your customers feeling the experience of your restaurant was unpleasant, regardless of the food.

In most restaurants the average table seats four people. In addition, you may have some tables for two, and a few for six or more people (depending on the size of your establishment). The average height of a table is twenty-four to twenty-six inches from the floor to the underside of the top. The top should be a minimum of one inch thick for stability. You may wish to have some round tables (particularly useful for tables seating six or more) in addition to standard square tops. Tables with square tops can be pushed together easily to form larger tables.

A heavy pedestal base is the most practical, since you don't have to worry about the legs becoming an interference. However, tables with legs are often more stable and easier to push together. A pedestal with spreading low legs may combine the best of both.

Choosing a table surface is often largely influenced by the kind of restaurant. Most casual and inexpensive restaurants don't use linens on the table, and so the table surfaces are of particular importance. Diners and family-style restaurants often rely on Formica-topped tables, which are easy to wipe down and keep clean. Some of them can be quite stylish, too.

For a more atmospheric quality, you might choose glass tops (which are cleaned with glass cleaner after every turn), resin-coated wooden tables, or even stone tops. Café Bernini in New York City, a reasonably priced but stylish Italian pasta restaurant, uses bare marble tabletops that are so beautiful they become a part of the decor. The rest of the furnishings are very simple.

Some restaurants use bare wood tabletops, often with place mats. If you choose this type of surface, you will need to be sure that the finish is sturdy. A fine French polish will not hold up, but a plastic finish will.

If you plan to use tablecloths, the tops can be very simple indeed. You can choose inexpensive plywood or flakeboard tops, since they will always be covered by a pad (which might be as simple as a folded undercloth). You can have these made yourself, or order them along with the bases from a dealer.

Tables should be large enough to hold the dishes served with enough room for diners to maneuver. They need not be great yawning spaces, but they should be large enough to hold several dishes for each diner, plus space in the middle.

Choosing good chairs is vital. They must be sturdy enough to withstand rough use but also comfortable. They need not offer the softness and support of an armchair (although these are sometimes used very successfully in luxurious restaurants)—you don't want your customers falling asleep in them or staying the entire evening. But your seating must be comfortable enough that the customer makes it through the average meal without wriggling around and needing to move or get up. The average chair seat rises sixteen to eighteen inches from the floor.

Other considerations when choosing a chair include decor compatibility and durability for cleaning. The variety of chair styles available is broad enough to suit the style of most kinds of restaurants. It only makes sense to choose a style that matches your decor. If you open a simple bistro, you will probably want simple, lightweight chairs. If your restaurant is in the grand luxe style, you will probably want to forgo the metal ice-cream chair in favor of a more substantial armchair.

If you plan to use upholstered chairs, be careful when choosing light-colored materials. You might wish to consider dark fabric tones or leatherlike upholstery. By the way, the chairs need not all match. It's probably not a good idea to mix styles, but you can vary the look slightly without anyone noticing, or you can make a feature of it. It's probably best to keep all the chairs at one table the same.

Bar furniture. Your bar area will in all likelihood reflect the decor of the dining room, and furnishings should be chosen with the larger scheme in mind. The bar furnishings certainly can be different from those in the dining room and may be more relaxed or casual. Tables and chairs must again be sturdy and capable of withstanding abuse due to lounging patrons, spilled alcohol, and cigarette burns. Bar chairs and tables are sometimes lower in height than those in the dining room. Stools must be sturdy and secure on their legs.

Tables and chairs may be bought new or used. Restaurant furniture dealers often have a fairly wide selection of both. If buying used, be sure to check the condition. Chairs must be sturdy and free of splinters and nicks. Tables must be sturdy and level as well. When choosing chairs, it's a good idea to have a few on trial for a week or two so that you can test their comfort. It's very hard to tell from a single brief sitting whether a chair will be comfortable for the duration of a meal.

Banquettes. Restaurants of all kinds use banquettes as a form of seating. They are most often seen as upholstered benches with backs lined along a wall. Tables and facing chairs are then placed in front.

Banquettes are a good way to use space efficiently, as you can arrange the tables closer together than if you were using a separate table and chairs. Customers often like them because they can survey the restaurant when seated against the wall. Banquettes come in a wide variety of styles and sizes. You can have them custom-upholstered or buy from dealer stock.

Some restaurants use a slight variation of the traditional banquette, taking wooden benches and lining them with pillows and a cushion. The Old Mill in Egremont, Massachusetts, uses two antique wooden settles with very high backs. They serve as decorative focal points in the dining room as well as practical seating.

Counter. A counter is another useful way of seating customers, and you don't have to have a diner of fast-food outlet to use one.

Outdoor furniture. Perhaps your restaurant has a lovely garden or a prime piece of wide sidewalk that you would like to use in the summertime for outdoor seating. The equipment you use will need to be specially suited to the great outdoors.

Tables and chairs must be able to withstand rain and sun. Therefore, you will probably consider those made of plastic or metal. Such outdoor dining tends to be pretty casual and thus is often fairly inexpensive. Outdoor furniture will also require a certain amount of maintenance and replacement, so try to figure in costs for annual refurbishing and replacement when doing your cost calculations.

China and tableware. No matter how simple your restaurant, you will require cutlery, napery, china, and table condiments. All of these elements should be coordinated with your decor, style of food, and budget.

The array of available goods is staggering. Restaurant trade shows are good venues for seeing all that's available. Salesmen will be happy to call as well. In fact, you may find yourself besieged by people trying to sell you goods. As with everything, shop around.

What should you be looking for when it comes to tableware? The first priority is durability. Everything will get hard use, so the sturdier the better. However, you may also need to balance sturdiness with style. You may not want all your tableware to look "industrial strength."

You'll also want to consider the food you serve and the atmosphere. Elegant food is best displayed on elegant china. Hearty and simple fare can stand up to heavy restaurant china.

Restaurant consultant Gary Goldberg tells the story of a client who was opening a jazz club in New Jersey. The food was to be simple and the atmosphere casual. He took her to a restaurant show where they saw all the equipment she was likely to need. They chose a stylish Formica tabletop with a wood-grain look and a black border. When choosing the china, the client fell in love with a simple white plate, but one made of a delicate bone china. Gary agreed that it was beautiful but endeavored to explain that the rather refined china didn't really fit the casual image of the club and the food to be served. "How could we go wrong with a white plate?" the client asked. A plain white plate can be almost infinitely varied, as Gary proved. He borrowed a plate, took it to the booth where they had chosen the table, and positioned it there. The client saw immediately that though she still loved the plate, it was far too formal for her restaurant.

If you are on a tight budget, you may be able to find china and silverware secondhand or as overstocks from restaurant supply dealers. This can be a significant savings if you can find a sufficient quantity in a pattern to serve your needs. Some people find the notion of mixing and matching china patterns and silver patterns charming. If you choose this route, you might try to find patterns that go well together or look only like slight variations of one another. Otherwise, it can be distracting to find several different and warring patterns on a table. This is particularly true for silverware when the weights of various patterns differ. It's distracting to have a heavy knife or spoon and a light fork.

QUANTITIES OF BASIC CHINA AND TABLEWARE NEEDED TO SERVE 50

China*

Bread and butter plates: 9 dozen
Soup bowls: 3 dozen
Dinner plates: 9 dozen
Salad and dessert plates: 15 dozen
Cups and saucers: 9 dozen

Tableware*

Dinner forks: 8 dozen
Salad and dessert forks: 12 dozen
Dinner knives: 8 dozen

Butter knives: 8 dozen
Teaspoons: 15 dozen
Soup spoons: 5 dozen

Glassware

Stemmed water glass or goblet: 12 dozen
All-purpose wineglass: 8 dozen
Stemmed dessert glass: 3 dozen

Miscellaneous Items

Salt and pepper shakers: 1 set per table plus a few extra
Salad bowls, if used: 6 dozen
Bread baskets: 3 dozen
Water pitchers: 6
Pepper mills: 3

* Note: China and tableware generally come packed in lots of three dozen. Tableware can usually be bought in any quantity, but breaking a lot may be reflected slightly in the price.

Even at franchise operations, very simple diners, and delis, china and tableware are required, though they are usually disposable. If you decide to go with disposables, be sure to check with local authorities regarding acceptable materials. The public is quickly becoming more aware of the problems of long-term disposal. Increasingly, we will be seeing restrictions as to the kind of acceptable disposable containers.

You might also base your choices more on the quality of goods than on cost. A cup of coffee tastes best out of china, next best out of paper, and worst out of Styrofoam. Hot foods that melt a Styrofoam container, even a little bit, take on the taste of the plastic. Not a pleasant experience.

Linens. You may not need to think about ordering linens

for the dining room if you plan on having bare tables and paper napkins. However, if your restaurant is a little more upscale and you intend to use tablecloths and cloth napkins, you will have to enter it into your budgeting.

There are two ways to go when it comes to linens. You can buy them and have them laundered by a service, or you can rent them from a laundry service. It is best, if you can afford it, to buy your linens, since you can control the quality of the goods. Laundry services generally have a very limited selection of linens, both in terms of quality and color range. If you are on a tight budget and have only a very small restaurant, you may consider laundering linens yourself, although this is most time-consuming. It will also affect your choice of materials. You probably won't have the time to iron linens, which means you will have to choose permanent-press materials, which are less absorbent and more difficult to get clean.

Whichever method you choose, keep in mind that the linens, along with the china and tableware, powerfully affect your guests' first impressions. If you can afford to, coordinate the linens with your decor. If your dining room is formal, use formal linens (this usually means white or pastels). If informal, you may want to go a more casual route, using cheerful colors or even patterns. In general, it's a good idea not to use solid, dark linens since they tend to fade and to show most stains. Pastel shades and patterned linens are often a good choice.

If you plan to use a laundry service, you must be sure to buy linens that are made for commercial use. Fabrics used at home cannot stand the repeated washings of a laundry service. The choice of material is largely a matter of cost. The most expensive and luxurious tablecloths and napkins are made of linen. They wash and iron well, always giving a crisp and finished look. All-cotton is the next most expensive, but overall, it is probably the most satisfactory material for the price. It can be washed in very hot water, irons well, and takes starch to give a crisp finish. Cotton is also very absorbent, which is a great help when it comes to spills. Cotton and synthetic blends are also frequently used for napkins and tablecloths. Such blends never look as crisp as linen and cotton, but they require very little or no ironing. All synthetic linens require little or no ironing as well, but they are not absorbent and tend to hold stains firmly.

When choosing linens, keep in mind the design of your china. Patterned china looks best over a plain tablecloth. Plain china looks great on patterned tablecloths.

LINEN NEEDS

For each meal, you will need the number of tables multiplied by the number of seatings at each table (some turn faster than others).

Cloths: Say you have ten tables. Seven of them turn three times a night, three only twice. You will thus need twenty-one cloths for the tables that turn three times, six for those that turn twice, for a total of twenty-seven cloths.

You may also use undercloths, which do not get changed with each turn, but once an evening. That gives a total of thirty-seven cloths.

Napkins: Seven of your ten tables seat four people, three seat six. If seven of the tables turn three times you will need 7 × 4 × 3, or 84 napkins. The three tables that turn twice will need 3 × 6 × 2 or 36 napkins. You will thus need a total of 120 napkins for each meal.

Next, you will need to know your laundry's delivery schedule. If they deliver every two days, you will need twice the number of linens figured for each meal. You should also figure on having an extra day's supply on your shelves, in case something happens and a delivery fails to arrive one day. You might also add a few extra napkins and tablecloths into your regular order to account for unforeseen uses and emergencies.

Service stations. Most restaurants have at least one, and often several, areas that the serving staff use as a base of operations outside the kitchen. This area often houses water pitchers, condiments, tableware, linens, serving trays, and sometimes the coffee service. It is an area that is essential for the serving staff, but must also be unobtrusive to diners.

There are a number of ways to treat a service station. It can be a table similar in style to the rest of the dining room placed in an out-of-the-way but visible place, convenient to the kitchen and dining room. It can become a part of the decor, as when the room features antique-style furniture and a serving board or hutch of a similar-looking style is used.

Sometimes work stations are placed behind a partition or wall so that they are not seen at all by diners. When obscured in this way, they are often functional tables, fitted with plenty of shelving for storage of linen, tableware, and china.

Decoration

How you decorate your restaurant is a matter of personal and perhaps business taste. You may wish to hire a restaurant consultant or interior designer, or you may wish to do it yourself. Whatever you choose, keep in mind that all colors, fabrics, and decorative touches should be pleasing to the majority of people likely to come into your establishment.

Colors. One foolproof way to choose colors is to start with a palette that harmonizes with food. Warm colors in general are a better choice than cool ones. Studies have shown that people eat more and return more frequently to restaurants that feature colors such as red, pink, orange, shades of brown, and deep colors. The atmosphere feels friendlier when warm colors are used instead of cool tones such as icy blues and light greens. Deep shades such as hunter green make people feel cozy. Stark contrasts of industrial gray, black, and white or other such combinations tend to work best when they are trendy. For the long haul, people generally feel better in a warm and inviting atmosphere.

Whatever colors you choose, make sure that the paint and wall coverings used are of good quality that can stand up to frequent brushing and even the occasional sponging or washing.

Flooring. The flooring you choose can be an essential part of your decor, but it is also as functional as almost any element. Many restaurants use carpeting, others use natural wood floors, ceramic tile, stone, terrazzo, or vinyl tiles.

Any material requires maintenance, some more than others. Carpeting may require more than any other, for it must be shampooed on a regular basis and replaced as it wears out. It also provides a warm atmosphere and serves to deaden sound, making for a quieter dining room. If you opt for carpeting, try to choose one that is not a solid color, as it is more likely to show dirt than a patterned carpet. It also pays in the long run to buy a sturdy carpet—often wool wears and cleans the best —that will stand up to hard use.

Wood floors can be very satisfactory surfaces as well. They provide a warm atmosphere, as does carpeting, yet they are easier to keep clean, since you can always give a quick mop when needed. Like carpeting, they need a certain amount of maintenance, particularly in the form of refinishing every few years, but the investment in wood floors is long-term. Hardwood floors, in particular, wear very well, and some of the modern finishes are quite durable. Wood floors are not as quiet as carpeted floors, but much more quiet than ceramic tile or stone.

Ceramic tile and stone floors are very durable, easy to care for, and can be extremely attractive. They are expensive to install, but maintenance is quite cheap once installed. Their rigidity can be hard on the legs and backs of serving staff who must stand on them for hours at a time. Such floors are also noisy, as they reflect rather than absorb sound. This is not much of a disadvantage, however, if you use other sound-deadening measures, such as table linen, upholstered chairs, draperies, and perhaps a porous ceiling. You might even want a noisy restaurant, as some seem to thrive with high noise levels.

Vinyl tile and sheet flooring are practical for a very simple and inexpensive restaurant. They are very easy to keep and are inexpensive to install. They do have to be replaced every few years, as they wear out quickly.

Electronic equipment. Few restaurants these days work without some sort of electronic restaurant equipment, including cash registers, calculators, and music systems. Cash registers come in a wide variety of styles with a staggering array of options to serve various needs and budgets. Some act as computers with precoded prices and the ability to transmit data to the kitchen and bar. You may need only a simple cash register and a hand calculator, or you may need an elaborate system. Sales representatives are happy to work with you to help define and meet your needs.

Depending on the kind of restaurant you open, you may or may not choose to have music. If you run a breakfast-and-lunch diner, music might serve as a distraction to your quick service and turnover.

If you serve leisurely dinners, you may value the pleasant atmosphere music can provide. It can help a sparsely filled dining room seem less empty.

Music can also set the tone of a restaurant. Soothing music has a relaxing effect. If your joint is hip and trendy, the music of the day may help convey your message as well as keep the energy level of the revelers high. Whatever your theme, you can reinforce it with appropriate music. Music also provides a sense of privacy by masking conversations from diners.

For all of these you will need a sound system, which, like the cash register, can be as simple or elaborate as your budget and requirements demand. Overall, a system that plays taped music is the best, since you make the tapes (or have them made for you) and control the tunes played. Relying on a radio station is a bad idea, unless it is a station specifically geared to restaurants. Even then, you have to put up with someone else's idea of what goes best in your restaurant and a hundred others nearby.

Decorative touches. Most restaurants have decorative

touches of some sort, be they flowers, objects, or both. Whatever you choose, be sure that the items can be kept clean easily. There is something unappetizing about looking up at a decorative item, such as the proverbial lobster and clam caught in the net of a fish restaurant, and seeing it covered with a thick layer of dust and cobwebs.

The Old Mill in South Egremont, Massachusetts, uses giant hand-blown jars of colorful peppers and olives preserved in oil atop tall pieces of furniture. The glass gleams and the vegetables look most inviting in their massed brilliance. They serve to whet the appetite by their colors and shape alone. The restaurant also has a collection of mandolins and antique wooden slicers mounted attractively along one wall.

Hail Columbia in Chatham, New York (see page 37), has a most effective display of antique mirrors along one wall of the dining room. There are at least a dozen, in varying sizes and shapes. Some are gilt, others are in warm wood tones. None are so large that diners feel self-conscious seeing themselves, but they have the effect of subtly enlarging the room and adding light to a windowless side of the room.

Hanging artwork has become a standard method of decorating a room. But beware of buying wholesale lots of mediocre or worse art just to put something on the walls. If you want to use pictures, consider using the work of a local artist or two who might be willing to let you show the work for free or at a modest fee. If you choose to do this, don't put prices on the pictures. If you are located in an active arts community, your restaurant can even serve as an informal gallery space by featuring the works of different artists on a regular or irregular basis.

Michele Miller of the Boiler Room Café in Southfield, Massachusetts (see page 38), chose to hang what she refers to simply as "good art" on the walls of the former boiler room and to have jazz piano music on weekends instead of spending heavily on other decorations and a fancy paint job. The faded paint and the artwork together to form a distinctive decor.

One of the most romantic restaurants in New York City uses murals as the main decorative element in the dining room.

When George Lang bought Café des Artistes, a rather faded landmark, in 1975, he had the Howard Chandler Christy murals of exuberantly beautiful frolicking nudes (commissioned for the restaurant in 1932) restored to their former glory. Today, they are the centerpiece of a restaurant that combines fine food with fine decor (see page 28).

Another contrast is provided by the Cowgirl Hall of Fame in New York (see page 32), which has a funky theme. This restaurant, associated with the actual Cowgirl Hall of Fame in Hereford, Texas, has a less-than-slick approach, using old rodeo posters, lamps made with images of vintage cowgirl get-togethers, and barbed-wire displays. Everywhere you turn, there's a bit of memorabilia that's definitely one of a kind.

Flowers are a lovely addition to any restaurant. Many restaurants use flowers and plants as their main decorative elements. There are few things that are as welcoming and appealing as beautiful arrangements of fresh flowers. Beware, however, since flower arrangements can be expensive and will need to be included in your operating budget.

If you look around, you may find a floral designer who is willing to provide you with regular arrangements at a reduced price for the privilege of the on-site advertising. Such barter arrangements often work very well, since beautiful flowers invariably elicit comments and questions from diners. If you use flowers on tables, keep arrangements simple and fresh. Check the condition of flowers every day and throw out those that appear to be fading.

Many restaurants use quantities of green plants as decoration as well. Plants can be used very successfully to provide a dramatic or calming ambience. Remember, however, that live plants need frequent care and upkeep. Half-dead or bedraggled plants look worse than none at all. If you choose to decorate with plants, consider hiring a company to keep them in good shape. Such companies are responsible for the care and feeding of plants, as well as their periodic replacement—necessary, given the harsh conditions of most restaurants.

Silk flowers and plants can be used, too, of course. If you choose to go this route, try to have a good designer make up your floral arrangements. It's expensive, but few things look worse in a restaurant than second-rate artificial flowers and plants. Artificial plants and flower arrangements will need to be cleaned frequently and replaced every six months or so, as they become soiled.

Rest Rooms

Washrooms are a necessary part of any restaurant. Your local health department may have regulations about various aspects of your rest rooms, but the most important thing is to make sure your rest rooms are well ventilated and can be kept clean easily. For many people, the success of the meal can be altered by the state of the rest rooms. They must be well stocked at all times, and kept tidy, in addition to being frequently cleaned. All appliances must work.

In some restaurants the rest room is merely a functional room. At others it can be decorated as an extension of the restaurant. For instance, at New York's Hot Diggity Bar and Grill an artist used colorful plastics to create padded doors with charming and fanciful full-size images of a man and a woman.

If your restaurant is located in a tourist area, the waiting area outside the rest room, or even the bathroom itself, can be a good place to display information about the area, and spots of local interest.

For many people, equipping and furnishing the space is one of the most exciting and challenging aspects of opening a restaurant. The first impression the restaurant makes on the customer must be both immediate and visual, but cannot be made by sacrificing the practical use of the working areas. Realizing your concept is a key task of the restaurateur, and it must be done with care and confidence.

CHAPTER

11

Your Staff

The restaurant business is a service industry that exists to please its customers. Thus, it is essential that your staff be well trained, pleasant, and ever mindful that they are there to serve. This applies to every member of the dining-room staff from the busers to the greeter or manager. It also applies to those in the kitchen whom the customer never sees.

Wait a second, you say. We all know of successful restaurants at which the staff are surly, impatient, or unhelpful. Durgin Park, almost an institution in Boston, has been known for generations to have the surliest waitresses in town. And yet, for this establishment, surliness has become almost a trademark, a part of the restaurant's "charm."

Well-established restaurants or those that provide a desired menu unique to an area may be able to get away with such service, but for most restaurants having a pleasant, well-trained staff can give the edge over the competition. In addition to making the place more appealing to visit, the staff that works well together is happier and tends to stay longer—which is good for the restaurant and for everyone, you included.

Establishing your expectations. When hiring staff, you should have a clear idea of your needs and wishes. Such considerations include how you want workers to act, look, and even think. That may sound dictatorial, but having these things in mind is actually a service to your employees. The best managers know what they want out of people and how to communicate it to them. It's much worse to have only vague notions of the responsibilities each staffer should have and then not be satisfied when he or she doesn't meet them.

As caterer Sean Driscoll of Glorious Food, a prestigious caterer based in New York, explains his sound philosophy for hiring any serving staff, "We're not tyrants, but I tell them, 'I don't care what you were before you came to me and I don't care what you do when you leave, but for those hours [you are here] you have to do what we say.' " For the hours that you employ someone, you must be able to depend on them to do the job required.

Paul McLaughlin, a captain at Le Bernardin in New York, puts it another way: "At five-thirty or six every evening you're onstage, so you have to put everything in your personal life aside." This philosophy applies to both kitchen and serving staff, for during the rush hours, everyone needs to be working as a team.

The Kitchen Staff

A good kitchen staff is vital to a smooth-running restaurant. The public rarely sees the kitchen workers, but without their labors you don't have a meal.

The head of the kitchen is the chef or head cook. Unless you intend to cook or run the kitchen yourself, this person is responsible for everything that goes on there. He or she consults with you regarding the menu, buying supplies, equipment, and the kitchen staff.

The responsibilities of chefs and cooks vary depending on

the kind of restaurant you operate. If yours is to be a very small restaurant with you or a partner in charge of the kitchen, your cooks probably won't need to be highly trained or able to delegate much responsibility. If yours is a franchise or full-service restaurant, you may have a kitchen manager who assumes much of the responsibility and who hires on-line cooks to carry out the simple meal preparations.

If you have anyone other than yourself in charge of the kitchen, that person will need to be able to get along with the other employees and to plan systems so that they can work together as a team. Enter any well-run restaurant during a rush and you will see all hands to the fore working in rhythm to produce meals. For this reason, if you have a chef or cook in charge, that person should be responsible for hiring other kitchen personnel such as cooks, preparation people, and dishwashers.

Expect frequent turnover in dishwashers. The work is boring, physically hard, and generally unrewarding. This is what makes a good dishwasher a jewel to find and hard to keep. Good dishwashers keep the kitchen staff constantly supplied with clean dishes, pots and pans, and utensils where they need them. They unglamorously keep the progression moving. You may need more than one, depending on the number of meals you serve. You may need one dishwashing station just for dining-room goods such as china, glassware, and tableware, and another for kitchen goods such as utensils, pots, and pans. A general dogsbody may also be responsible for keeping the kitchen relatively clean during a shift—taking out trash and garbage, cleaning floors, and other tasks.

The Service Staff

Dining-room staff requirements are, in general, the same for just about all restaurants. The numbers will certainly vary, and you may have extensions of the basic staff, but basically you will need to fill positions for a room manager, waiting staff, bus personnel, and bartenders, if you serve wine or liquor. The number of people you will need depends on the number of seats.

The most important staff person is the manager, who will most likely be you or a partner. The manager, who may be called hostess, host, or maître d', runs everything. He or she is responsible for taking reservations, organizing seating, greeting guests and seating them, distributing menus, supervising the dining-room staff (which sometimes means orchestrating their movements), occasionally taking orders, acting as liaison between kitchen and dining room, sometimes operating the cash register, and generally keeping an eye on the operating process to ensure that guests have a good time.

In pressured situations, the manager must be able to fulfill any function in the dining room and appear unruffled, friendly, and in control, making it all look easy. The humorist Art Buchwald describes the perfect maître d'hôtel as someone who should "greet you as a friend but not bother with you afterwards—as a friend would."

If you hire someone to be your manager, do so with especial care. A manager must be organized, tactful, friendly, quick-witted, and calm. He or she must be able to step in when a crisis develops and do what needs to be done, from serving a meal to calming the ruffled feathers of customers or staff.

Servers are next in importance, since they do much of the actual servicing of patrons. Servers usually announce specials (should you choose to give them orally), take orders (both of which may be done by the maître d'hôtel, or manager), deliver orders to the kitchen and bar, receive orders from the kitchen and bar, do last-minute preparation such as plating and dressing salad and pouring coffee, and deliver the food. In some restaurants servers take orders but another person actually delivers the food. They answer the customer's questions and see to it that the delivery of each part of the meal is handled smoothly.

Servers must be able to work in concert with other staff such as busers, bartenders, chef and prep people, and the manager. If at all possible, you will want servers who are organized, can get along easily with fellow workers, and are pleasant and patient with customers.

Buspeople—and they can be male or female—work as assistants to the servers. Generally, their duties include setting and clearing the table of dishes during the meal. They often are responsible for bringing bread and butter, or whatever else goes on the table before the ordered dishes arrive. They also may help the waiter or waitress bring food from the kitchen and serve.

Some restaurants break up some of the serving and clearing tasks. They may have someone who makes sure the tables have water and rolls. This person also often takes orders for and serves coffee and tea. He or she can also relay messages to the server, who may be very busy with other tables, and generally fill in when a busperson or server needs a hand. Keeping track of these sorts of details makes guests feel pampered.

The Employment Procedure

The procedure for hiring people for all staff positions is simple. First, you have to find them, have them fill out a simple application form, and then interview them. The result of your review of the application and the interview will determine who you hire more than any other factor. But first, you have to find prospective candidates.

Most staff positions, including waiters and waitresses, buspersons, preparation cooks, and dishwashers, can often be filled through word-of-mouth advertising. Most of the restaurant owners I have spoken with have found this method very satisfactory. They find that once you have a few good people, they tend to know other good people. The word of a good restaurant gets around and tends to draw well-qualified people as well.

The word-of-mouth approach, however, may not work when you are first starting out, so there are several other methods you can employ. The simplest is to post a sign on your window saying NOW HIRING or some such. You can also place advertisements in the classified section of your local newspaper. You can contact local vocational schools and trade schools featuring a food service department. If you live near a college or university, the job board is often a good place to put an ad card.

When it comes to the more skilled jobs, such as cook or chef, assistant chefs (should you need them), and manager, the same methods of word of mouth and print advertising usually work well. You might also try advertising in specialty magazines geared to the food trade or professional cooking schools or hotel management schools.

THE APPLICATION FORM

An application form for employment can be quite simple and should be straightforward. Basically, you want to know the person's name, age, address, previous experience, and any references they might have. After hiring an individual, you will also want to keep his or her application form on file, as it initiates the paper trail that is required of an employer for tax and other purposes.

The application form might look something like this:

Date of application:

Name:
Address:
Telephone:

Age:

Position applied for:

Previous employment:
[Please cite name of restaurant, your duties, the period you worked, your reason for leaving, and your supervisor's name.]

1.

2.

3.

4.

References:
[Name and Address, Telephone, Relationship]

1.

2.

3.

Applicant's signature:_____

———————————————————

The Interview

Sizing up potential employees firsthand is vital to good hiring decisions. Anybody can be made to look good on paper, but judging someone's personality can only be done in person. Personality is crucial in most restaurant positions, particularly those in the dining room.

Personality and professional qualifications vary for the different positions.

Serving staff. Servers are your primary link with the public. They must therefore be presentable in appearance. They must be well groomed, which means they must be clean from fingernails to hair to clothing. A neat appearance makes a difference to customers, even if only on a subliminal level.

Beyond appearance, you will want to look for certain characteristics. Serving staff must be friendly, willing to smile, and able to speak with confidence. Diane Selby says of her serving staff, "They have to look happy. If they don't smile, they already put a damper on the food."

Serving staff should be enthusiastic and willing to work as part of a team. People with large egos or an attitude that the world owes them something will probably have trouble getting along with other staff members and may take out their frustrations on customers. The result will be a restaurant whose atmosphere is frayed at the edges.

One small-seeming element to consider is the person's handwriting. Unless you plan to have a computer system for communicating orders, your servers will need legible handwriting so that the kitchen staff can decipher their orders. This is easy to tell from the application form.

How important is experience when it comes to serving staff? There are several answers.

Some people feel that hiring people with a lot of restaurant experience is important. Often the thinking is that such employees require little or no training and can step right in and do a job. Other restaurateurs have found that hiring people with little experience makes it easier to teach them their methods. Those who go with the little-experience approach often feel that a person's attitude and willingness are more important than their current skills (the other school counters that real pros can fit in and adapt quickly to the owner's needs and wants). Whichever approach you feel most comfortable with, the more you can communicate your wishes to serving employees, the better they can be trained and work together.

The one position that most people agree must be filled by someone with training or experience is that of bartender. Bartenders need to know how to mix any kind of drink ordered, understand portioning, get along with customers, and be able to work efficiently with the serving staff. They must be friendly and welcoming to customers and staff alike.

Kitchen staff. Interviewing people for kitchen positions is quite like that of the dining-room staff, with a few exceptions. While the kitchen staff need not be as carefully groomed as the serving staff, they must exhibit clean habits or be able to adapt to your requirements. People who handle food should have clean fingernails, should not habitually run their hands through their hair or constantly touch their skin. If they smoke, it must be done away from food in an out-of-the-way area or outside, during breaks only.

Kitchen staff must be reliable. You can't have your pantry person, or worse, your chef, fail to show up for a shift, leaving you shorthanded. Unfortunately, restaurant staff are often known for not appearing or for leaving on sudden notice. You may well find yourself filling in at a variety of stations from time to time. Don't expect many of the people you interview to have a long history at one restaurant.

Kitchen staff should be able to adapt quickly to the needs of your kitchen. People handling food must be organized, since split-second timing is the order of the day. You also don't need people who are temperamental and difficult to work with. The classic cliché about chefs being temperamental may in some cases be true, but that doesn't mean you have to employ such chefs, unless you can be assured that they can work efficiently and well with other kitchen staff.

Staff Dynamics

A smooth-working staff can be one key to long-term success. Be a little patient, however, as it may take awhile for people and systems to settle in to a good working relationship.

Terry Moore of the Old Mill feels very strongly that the staff must be able to work together in order for the work to get done and the customer to be satisfied. "I stress that all the time. I won't allow friction," he says. On the other hand, he also acknowledges that it takes time to develop a smooth flow with the staff. At first you're almost bound to have people jockeying for position and to have friction between the dining-room and kitchen staff.

Since you can't tell just how people will work out from the beginning, there is almost certainly going to be some juggling of personnel as well. You may discover that someone who seemed just right when hired turns out to have a poor attitude or can't gracefully take the pressure of waiting tables and servicing customers. Such people have to be replaced. You may not be able to do it right away, as it's often difficult to find personnel. Yes, good help is often hard to find. However, the more your restaurant becomes known as a good place to work, the more you will have the cream of people from which to choose. Good staff want to work at well-run, pleasant restaurants.

Remuneration

You want to attract good people who will pay back your investment in them. One of the best ways to develop a loyal working staff is to pay them fairly.

These days a fair pay scale often means more than just a higher wage than some of your competition. It includes how you schedule increases, how you handle tips, and what sorts of fringe benefits you provide. Until fairly recently the notion of benefits was practically unheard of for restaurants, but today the more fringe benefits you can provide, the better your chances for attracting loyal staff.

The restaurant business runs according to several sets of pay standards. Full-time workers are paid differently from part-time, while servers usually work at a different rate from kitchen staff. Most restaurant staff work for an hourly wage, with the possible exceptions being the chef and manager, both of whom might work on a salary.

To determine fair rates in your area, check out a number of sources for information. Talk to other restaurateurs and ask what rates they pay. Contact your local restaurant association, chamber of commerce, or state employment agency for information. When interviewing, ask employees what they've been making. Read the employment section in local newspapers and see what rates are advertised. You also have to keep the federal minimum-wage law in mind.

To attract trained employees, you will have to offer the going rate, or even a little more, but this will vary from job to job. Serving staff, who earn tips in addition to their wages, generally earn a lower hourly wage, often around half of what those who work behind the scenes earn. The government even acknowledges this discrepancy in the minimum-wage law. What the government allows and what good people command are two different things, but the ratio is still a good guideline for paying servers.

Policies regarding tipping vary from restaurant to restaurant as well. Many restaurateurs feel that the best servers deserve all their tips alone (or shared with their bus personnel). Others feel that this can be detrimental to the team spirit necessary to a smooth-running operation.

Certain stations often have better tables, the best tippers may always sit at one table or another, and the large parties (who invariably tip badly) tend to be relegated to certain areas—all these are factors. To address the inequities these circumstances may present, you can do one of several things.

You can rotate your best servers so that they all have the opportunity to work the best stations. Or you can pool the tips so that everyone goes home with the same amount of money each night. You can divide the room so that each station has some good tables.

Terry Moore strongly feels that one of the reasons his staff works well as a team is that the tips are pooled and divided equally. He feels that squabbles are greatly reduced. "It's all one team and everybody walks out of here at the end of the night with the same money. And that's important." Everyone works hard for the good tips. If some servers fall well below the par of the others, they can be replaced.

You will have to pay kitchen staff at a better rate, since they usually receive no gratuities. Your head cook or chef may be on salary, may have a percentage of earnings (profit sharing), or may work on a standard hourly basis, depending on the type of operation you run. Assistant cooks may have the same sort of arrangement, albeit at a lower rate, if they are highly trained. Dishwashers are usually the least well paid, as their jobs require the least skill.

Try to have your rates in place before you hire staff. You may have to be flexible on this, as you discover what people are willing to work for and how your business changes in the months after opening.

Be prepared to make frequent staff adjustments. It's almost impossible in the beginning to know just when your busiest times will be and how many people you will need working at those times. Rates can be adjusted once you see how well business is doing and how well customers tip.

Basic wages and tips are not the only element in determining pay scales. You also have to be prepared to increase pay scales for loyal and good workers. Experienced workers are worth more than inexperienced ones. They tend to be faster and make fewer mistakes. However, as inexperienced help learns, they should be rewarded commensurately.

It is thus a good idea to establish increases at specific intervals. For instance, people just starting out might be put on a trial level. After, say, a month that level would be raised. After three months, it would be raised again, and again at six months, nine months, or a year. At the end of each interval an employee's performance is rated and the pay increased if the performance is satisfactory. Once an employee has been with you a year or more, you should review performance annually, or as needed.

Not every employee will fit neatly into the interval review system. Occasionally you may find yourself with someone whose work quickly proves outstanding. This person should be rewarded accordingly. You may want to shorten the intervals.

Whatever method you choose, try to establish an advancement policy. This gives a sense of security to prospective employees.

Benefits

As mentioned, benefits are becoming an important part of the restaurant industry. They provide incentives for good employees to stay. The longer you can keep good staff as a team, the better your restaurant will run. Constantly changing employees is expensive in time, money, and service to customers.

If your restaurant is in a seasonal community, you may have to rely almost solely on transient seasonal help. If this is the case, you won't have to concern yourself with setting up structures for paying for health insurance, vacation, and sick pay.

However, if you run a year-round restaurant, providing benefits is cheaper in the long run. Such benefits as hospital and major medical insurance, sick pay, and vacation pay can be offered after a certain interval of employment to full- or part-time employees (the latter are usually defined as those who regularly work twenty hours or more each week but less than forty).

Providing total health insurance is often prohibitively expensive for restaurants, especially those that are not yet profitable. What many do is offer inclusion in a group plan in which you pay a portion of the costs, and the employee contributes the rest. The amount you pay can be tied to the amount of time an employee has been with you, or can be a straight percentage of the cost from the day he or she accepts the plan.

As in any business, vacation pay is usually determined by length of service. In the restaurant business it is most common to award it after a year of employment to both full-time and part-time workers. The amount of pay is determined by the amount of hours worked during the year in the case of part-time workers and by the salary in the case of full-time employees.

The privilege of sick pay is one that is easily abused, so make requirements for it fairly tight. Generally, a worker is allowed a certain number of sick days for each interval worked, perhaps a day a quarter. Limit the amount to a certain number of days per year. Someone who really needs the time and whose work you value can be given more as needed.

Staff Training

Anyone you hire will need to be taught the way you want things done. This is true from the chef to the dishwasher and from the manager to the busperson. The amount of training for each job varies quite a lot, however.

A chef with whom you are placing your trust to create a special menu and whom you expect to hire and supervise the kitchen staff should require little in the way of teaching. Indeed, to do so with well-qualified people can be insulting.

It is appropriate, however, to explain how you want things generally run, and what your expectations are. Anything less is really not fair to any employee. Buying procedures and the mechanics of standardized recipes should be explained as well. In the case of franchised restaurants, a manual for cooks and managers should be provided.

Serving staff may need considerable training, depending upon the labor pool available or on your wishes. Before you first open, it's a good idea to have at least a training session or two for the serving staff as a whole so that everyone is equally familiar with the procedures at your restaurant. Lettuce Entertain You, a Chicago restaurant group that owns twenty restaurants, runs training sessions lasting a week for new employees. Before they open a new restaurant, they rehearse staff for three weeks.

When the top-rated Le Bernardin restaurant in New York first opened in 1986, everyone from regular customers to the New York press marveled at the flawless service of the staff. Maguy Le Coze, co-owner with her husband, Gilbert, remembers that they trained waiters and captains for a month. "They had notebooks. They were tested," she says.

General training sessions serve several purposes. They are an opportunity for you or your manager to explain your restaurant's policies regarding everything from how a guest is greeted to selling the menu to serving the food. Instead of telling each person, you can show the group how you want dishes presented, how to portion certain foods such as desserts, which servers sometimes plate, how you want the tables set and cleared, and other specifics.

Such sessions are also an opportunity for the staff to meet and get to know you and one another. The demonstrations should be serious and instructive, but also fun. It's a time to show the kind of atmosphere you wish to develop. A general session involving trained and untrained personnel should not last more than an hour or so. It's a good idea to provide refreshments afterward, too. More specialized sessions can be conducted for inexperienced people needing more instruction.

In addition to training, which given the nature of rushed openings may be less leisurely and thorough than you may wish, you should also provide a thorough job description. Give this to each employee on being hired and have them read it and refer to it as needed.

Once your business is operating, you'll probably want to train new people individually. The standard method is to have someone work on a trial basis of a week or so under an experienced person. They learn as they go, each day taking on new responsibilities.

A FEW POINTS TO CONSIDER WHEN TRAINING

Demeanor

Dining-room staff should be pleasant and helpful, but unobtrusive. If a problem develops, explain the situation and apologize to the patron.

Premeal Preparation

Waiting staff should always know who gets which dish. If a server has to ask who ordered the fish (or chicken—whatever), diners tend to wonder how well he or she is paying attention and how much care is being given to their meals.

Timing

All diners should be served within a few moments of the same time. All meals should coordinate courses so that the people who order appetizers are not served as their companions' entrées arrive.

Serving Techniques

When possible, dishes should be served from the left and cleared from the right. Plates should be glided to the place at a low angle instead of plunked down. Plates should not be cleared until all diners at the table have finished. Plates should also be removed as unobtrusively as possible.

Coordinating Staff Duties

Since the serving of a table usually requires the efforts of several people, often beginning with the manager, maître d', or captain, and continuing to the waiting staff and busing staff, their efforts must be coordinated. Each person must know his or her duties and the timing involved for each step. The manager, maître d'hôtel, or captain often direct the waiters and waitresses, and they in turn direct the actions of the busers and any others working with them.

Staff Meetings

Once your restaurant is operating, it's a good idea to conduct brief staff meetings before each meal. This is the time to explain any specials on the menu as well as notes and comments on certain dishes you want featured. It's also a good time to take staff suggestions and to make announcements and set the general tone for the session as well as to check uniforms or grooming of the waiting staff.

Dressing the Part

Most restaurants require that employees dress uniformly. This is done as a service to customers, who automatically see and evaluate the staff, and to give a look to a restaurant.

The variety in restaurant dress is almost endless, ranging

from theme costumes to traditional formal attire to the simplest of coordinated outfits. Many restaurants find that a simple dress code is easiest on the staff.

This usually involves coordinating colors such as a black skirt or trousers with a white blouse or shirt. Often a coordinated or matching tie of some sort completes the look. You may also provide an apron, which might be as simple as a white towel or something more elaborate, say with the restaurant's name imprinted. Such a dress code is easy for employees to provide and easy for them to keep neat and clean.

If your restaurant has a strong theme or is a franchise, more elaborate uniforms might be required. When this is the case, you will probably have to buy them for employees, who are then responsible for their upkeep. Sometimes the cost of uniforms is deducted from pay.

Kitchen employees usually dress in white uniforms, often provided by the owner (though with the cost deducted from the employees' pay). They must be kept clean. Kitchen help should also be provided with a minimum of one fresh apron each day. This will come out of your linen budget.

Feeding staff. Most restaurants expect employees to arrive to work, not to eat. Others provide a staff meal before the first seating or at the end of the shift. Others allow employees to eat from the menu at the end or beginning of the shift.

If you choose to let employees eat from the menu, it's best to give them a few options, not free rein. Restaurants that provide seated staff meals often use the time as an informal staff meeting to discuss day-to-day business and operations.

Dry runs. One excellent way to make sure your staff is in shape for opening day is to schedule a few dry runs. Perhaps you might want to invite friends or investors down for a meal (usually on the house) or to schedule a private party (or several) prior to opening. Such events give the staff a real workout without the pressure of worrying about return custom. It's understood that these are unoffical openings and that systems may still need to be worked out.

Staff Scheduling

Some or even most of your serving staff and some of the kitchen staff may work part-time. That way you can schedule people for the busiest shifts without having everyone on the payroll when not needed. Many restaurants find that they need extra waiting, busing, and dishwashing staff on weekends or during other busy times.

You will probably want to schedule your most experienced servers for the busiest meals. For most restaurants this is dinner, when most really good servers are most willing to work —tips are best. Keep at least one serving person on call if possible for those times when someone reports in sick at the last moment or simply doesn't show up.

You may also find that servers will swap shifts with one another to accommodate their schedules. In general, it's best if they go through you or your manager, since you are the one responsible for the mix of staff at any one time. People who take advantage of others by trading off shifts frequently should be reviewed carefully. Constant juggling by the same people causes disruption among other staff members and suggests that the person doesn't really care about the job.

Working out a scheduling pattern that works best for your restaurant takes time and experience. Keeping daily records of the number of people served at each meal is a good way to establish overall patterns. You can use these to project general trends for your business, being sure to take into account the vagaries of season and day of the week.

Management Techniques

One of the most important things you can do to assure the success of your restaurant is to develop good techniques for managing your employees. Managing workers well and efficiently helps enormously to provide a pleasant working atmosphere. Your turnover is likely to be lower and the efficiency of your staff is likely to be greater. Both of these elements are reflected in the way customers are treated. Patrons who have experienced a pleasant meal are more likely to become repeat customers.

Continuous supervision of your employees after training is an ongoing process. It takes awhile for people to develop a rhythm, and they sometimes need more than one instruction to master certain tasks or procedures.

As things progress you may find that certain people need more guidance in some areas. For instance, some people may have too heavy or light a hand when serving, and you will have to monitor them, reminding them to cut down or increase portions, keeping them consistent. You may have to remind serving staff to keep an eye on all their tables and to assess their customers' needs continuously. Others may need reminders about your preferred methods of serving and clearing of dishes. Since the restaurant business is one of details, you will be called on constantly to monitor such seeming nonessentials.

Don't hesitate to criticize when needed, but if at all possible do it in a constructive manner by demonstrating a better way to do something and by being firm but good-humored. This doesn't mean you can't occasionally get angry, but it should only be for something that truly warrants it and it should be infrequent. Your behavior should be consistent. That way your staff knows that you are the demanding but fair leader.

In addition to all the good techniques you can develop, there are a few management don'ts you should follow, too. Don't show favoritism among your staff. Of course, some employees will be better or more attuned to your personality than others, but try not to let your preferences show.

As with any business, it's probably a bad idea to get romantically involved with one of your employees, as it is only likely to breed friction among the others.

Don't allow your doubts and fears to show. This doesn't mean you need to be unrealistically happy all the time, but you should exhibit a professional confident demeanor.

One crucial element in good management is creating a team spirit. There are a number of ways of doing this, but they all hinge on making staff members feel they are important to the operation. Everyone needs praise for a job well done. Tell your staff how much you appreciate their good service or when they've done a particularly good job. Reward them occasionally with a party. Make a big deal of birthdays. Give bonuses when warranted.

During a rush or on one of those days when everything seems to go wrong, things can get tense. Thanks-yous can be forgotten and tempers can be strained. This is inevitable on occasion, especially in a new operation. When this happens, be sure to thank staff afterward for any extra effort they've given to make things work. You may find that a celebratory glass of champagne or some such treat helps smooth things along after a rocky patch.

There are lots of good management techniques that help keep a happy team, including the ones you will develop for your particular situation. Terry Moore has one that clearly works well—his chef at the Old Mill has been with them for eight years. "We try to recognize what the employees do. They work very hard, and it's very much a team spirit. We keep the job exciting."

One of the ways they do this is to occasionally take the staff away from the restaurant. Often they schedule the trip around a food show. "We'll go to the Boston show, say, and stay overnight and go to dinner and go for breakfast somewhere in the morning and make it a real fun time. We love to go to restaurants which are new and exciting, places that are in vogue, to see what's happening." It pays dividends in many ways: staff morale is kept high, they get fresh ideas from seeing how others do it, and they have a sense that they belong to a unique organization.

Terry also finds that one way to keep the staff happy is to pay attention to their needs. "I always want the employees in the kitchen to feel like I'm doing the best for them." One way to do this, he finds, is to provide them the best in the way of equipment. When a piece of much-used equipment, such as the broiler, begins to show wear, they replace it promptly, before anything can happen to cause a breakdown.

Terminating employees. On occasion you will have to end someone's employment even after you've tried to work things out. This may come as a result of a number of factors, including poor performance or attitude, frequent lateness, stealing, or absence. Different situations require different approaches.

In no case should you lose your temper, no matter how difficult or rude the employee acts. In general, it is best to be straightforward and honest without being cruel.

Try not to let a bad situation linger. This doesn't mean that the first time performance slips you fire an employee. Try to make the situation work and give advance warnings of possible termination. However, once this has been done and things still aren't working, it is often no help to the person to be kept on in the hope that another job will be found or that he or she will realize that this job isn't suited to him or her. It's bad for performance and morale—both the employee's and the rest of the staff's. Of course, it's not always practical to get rid of a staff member if you don't have someone else to take their place. In some instances you'll have to weigh whether it's better to be shorthanded temporarily than have to suffer the consequences of a poor employee.

There are several good policies to follow once you actually do fire an employee. First, keep a written record of the case, noting the reasons and explanations. Second, have the person's paycheck drawn up. Third, don't fire the person in public, do it in your office or a quiet out-of-the-way place. Fourth, get to the point quickly rather than meandering around the issue. Fifth, before you hand over the check, ask if the employee has anything to add. The employee's observations may be useful or not, but you can use them as you see fit. Make sure the employee turns over any restaurant property, such as uniform or keys, before leaving.

You may choose to give an employee notice of termination, allowing him or her to work until a specified date, such as the end of the next pay period. This usually works well in businesses in which employees need to finish up projects or hand over work to others. In the restaurant business it can be quite tricky, since employees deal directly with the public and job performance tends to take a nosedive when one is under notice of termination. This may not be quite so important for the janitor or dishwasher (although you may experience record breakage and noise), but it's crucial for service employees.

Then again, most of us find something cruel in shoving someone out on the street. You will have to find an approach that suits your personality and the given situation.

CHAPTER

12

Getting the Word Out

There is a one more essential part of the plan that cannot be left to chance—namely, the marketing of your restaurant.

In many ways all public aspects of the restaurant—including the location, menu, food, service, and decor—will help promote your establishment. It is certainly desirable, however, to have a head start on the word of mouth by letting your community know you are there even in advance of opening.

It's unrealistic to expect that on the first day open you will be serving to standing-room-only crowds. Before you get to the stage where repeat business fills the house regularly, you would do well to develop some strategies for getting the word out about your restaurant. This effort should probably include public relations to establish yourself as a part of your community, and advertising, of which there are several kinds.

We'll start with the most secure and least expensive form of promotion, public relations.

Community Relations

The best thing you can do for your restaurant when first starting out is to get involved in the community. By building goodwill there, you can help build a strong community base to support the restaurant during the lean times as well as the flush ones. This is true even if you are located in a resort community and are open only for the tourist season. The more people know and recommend your establishment—whether it's an everyday diner or the kind of restaurant they go to once a year for a special event—the better for your business.

To build community support you have to get involved. Many methods exist, and you may have your own already planned or in place, but the following are a few suggestions.

- Make the acquaintance of the editor of the local newspaper.
- Propose a good rate for the Christmas party for the local town or city officers.
- Offer a few free meals as door prizes to charity events.
- Join the local chamber of commerce or other business group.
- Add your name, and if possible, give time to community events such as town fairs.
- Have your restaurant donate extra food to programs for the homeless or other social-service agencies.
- Participate in the town's beautification program.
- Contribute to local fund drives.

Perhaps the most important aspect of community relations is your treatment of your customers. It's easy if you are located in a resort community to fall into the habit of treating tourists or summertime visitors differently from the local people, but if you possibly can, try to treat everyone as special patrons. Make sure to train your staff to do the same.

Local people who are treated well will recommend your place to their friends and any travelers they meet as well as make it a regular stop for themselves. Tourists and seasonal residents will recommend it to their friends at home as well as make a point of returning when in the area.

Chincoteague, a fishing and resort town on the Eastern Shore of Virginia, is packed with restaurants to service the tourist industry. Some of its eating places make revealing points about how to deal with custom.

Most of Chincoteague's restaurants are located on the roads most traveled to the beach or motels. With few exceptions, the turnover of these restaurants is about every two years. The four longest lasting are part of the community. The Channel Bass Inn is a gourmet restaurant and inn where few local residents eat but which they can recommend because of the community life of the owners. The other three are local hangouts that also cater to tourists and out-of-town commercial fishermen. Pony Pines, Chincoteague Inn, and Bill's are open year round and are the sorts of places you might expect to see a weekly Rotary Club gathered for lunch. Pony Pines for years had the hottest (and perhaps only) jukebox and dance floor in town; the Chincoteague Inn has the most pool tables and best view; and Bill's specializes in early meals. Breakfast starts at four in the morning for the local fishermen, and the restaurant is all locked up by eight in the evening, when the last of the iced tea has been poured and the empty pie plates scraped clean. Tourists who bother to ask local residents where to go are almost invariably directed to one of the four.

Advertising

There are lots of kinds of advertising. The best is without doubt the recommendations of satisfied customers. Word-of-mouth advertising is a testament to a well-run restaurant, for it shows that people enjoy the service they receive, the atmosphere of your establishment, the food they've eaten, and the value of the experience. If you strive to be the best of your kind in your area, the word will get around.

The ebullient restaurateur Wolfgang Puck, of Spago's in

Los Angeles, prefers to use any budget he might otherwise put into advertising into vintage champagne. He uses it to toast the birthdays of frequent and favored customers. Talk about garnering wonderful advertising . . . but then his restaurant perennially is one of the hottest in town.

Getting your restaurant established enough for the word to get around takes precious time, and you might want to consider employing some other kinds of advertising to get started. There are all kinds of things you can do to get your name out in the public and build your reputation, and not all of them cost much money.

You might want to start with a local newspaper. Most papers are looking for stories, particularly about local businesses. Call and ask for a business reporter. See if you can interest this person in doing an article on your restaurant. You'll want to show how it fits into the community, what it provides that the community needs, how it differs from the competition, and anything else you can think of that sets you apart.

Hail Columbia arranged for the local paper to run a brief article and recipe from the chef once a week. The newspaper didn't have anything like it; it added interest to its pages, and the restaurant and chef were kept before the public in each weekly issue.

Once you've been open a little while, you might want to try to get reviewed in local newspapers and magazines. Call up the editors and tell them that you are interested in being reviewed at their convenience. The Boiler Room Café doubled its business when *The New York Times* and *New York Observer* gave favorable reviews. People sought the out-of-the-way restaurant and flocked in, reviews in hand.

Many talk-radio shows have restaurant reviewers as well. When they give their on-the-air opinions, they can alert and sway thousands of listeners at a go. Call up the radio stations, or send a copy of a publicity letter or brochure announcing your opening. You can't depend on getting reviewed, but if you do, it can give a good boost.

In addition to reviews and community sponsorship there

is one very simple thing you can do to further your public relations. Keeping a guest book in which you encourage patrons to sign and comment is a great way to track where guests come from and what they particularly liked and disliked about your restaurant. If several people comment on the lusciousness of your desserts, you know unequivocally that it's a strong part of your menu. A guest book is also one of the few ways the chef receives direct and effective commentary.

People tend to be laudatory when making comments, but sometimes you can read between the lines to see where problems might lie. If no one ever praises the service, you might want to evaluate your staff and their methods.

Finally, a guest book provides a surprising amount of entertainment for the guests who sign, as well as for you. We all like to see the distances people have traveled, and to see if we know anyone else who has enjoyed a restaurant as much as we have. It is also useful in determining where you might wish to advertise. Perhaps the most fun comes from the comments of the clever and witty among us.

Print advertising. Running an ad in the newspaper is the most direct print method for presenting your restaurant to the public. The advertising department of any newspaper will be delighted to hear from you. If you live in a small town, they will probably have contacted you already.

Some advertising departments are more creative than others and may actually be able to offer advice on developing an ad campaign. If not, perhaps your own creativity will help you develop a concept. You can also contact an advertising agency whose staff handles every aspect, from developing ideas to the execution and page-ready makeup of print advertisements. An advertising agency may also be able to advise you and develop other forms of coordinated advertising, including radio ads, promotions, and giveaways. Using an advertising agency can be very expensive, however, and many restaurateurs choose to get along without one.

If you don't hire the services of an agency, you will need to be able to prepare an ad for insertion into publications. If you've hired a graphic artist to design your logo and menu, this person should know how to prepare an ad for publication.

First, you will need to compose the copy, the information you want relayed. It may sound simplistic, but the two elements you absolutely must include are your hours of operation and your location. After that, it's pretty much up to you. You'll probably want to identify the kind of food you serve, and you might want to entice people in with a special opening promotion or catchy copy. Whatever you say in an ad must be truthful. Leave out the hyperbole.

THINGS YOU SHOULD KNOW ABOUT PREPARING AN AD FOR PUBLICATION

Considering the amount of time, effort, and money you spend on getting your restaurant under way, it only makes sense to put the same kind of care into preparing print ads. There are several things to keep in mind when gathering information and putting it together.

Don't rely totally on the advice of your designer. Have some ideas in mind before you approach the person. You should be flexible and respect the judgment of your designer, but the more guidance you give regarding what you want, the happier you will be with the result. One way to get ideas is to scour newspapers and magazines for ads you like and clip them. Try to analyze why you like them and what impression they left. Present your favorite clips to your designer and explain what you like about them.

Any ad should contain a distinct image. This can be your restaurant's logo, a drawing or photo of the place, or special lettering of the name. Whatever you choose, it should be simple enough that a reader of the publication will remember it.

The overall design of the ad should also be simple

enough that the copy is easy to read. Too much copy confuses the reader and muddies an otherwise clear first impression.

Choose a typeface that is easy to read and appropriate to the style of your restaurant. If yours is a sleek modern establishment, Gothic or fancy-script lettering will give the wrong impression to the reader. If, on the other hand, yours is a romantic restaurant, you might want to convey that with a flowery typeface.

When planning an ad, have your designer make an over-all master design in which certain elements of the copy can be changed for subsequent runs. It's unnecessary and expensive to design a completely new ad every time you run it. Besides, it may take readers a few times to notice your ad.

Be sure to check the spellings of any dishes with foreign names that you include in your ad. It looks unprofessional to have misspellings in printed copy. To this end, be sure to proofread the ad once your designer has had it set into type. If you rely on the services of the newspaper or magazine to design your ad and set the type, be sure to proof it before they print it. Chances are good that the in-house art department will be less scrupulous than you or your own designer.

Magazine ads can be another good source of customers. Advertising in magazines can be quite expensive, however, so it's wise to choose your outlet carefully.

Regional magazines geared to your area can be a great value. To find out which magazines are most likely to benefit you, call the advertising offices of a select few. Ask for their demographic studies. By studying the kind of people who read the magazine, you may be able to tell if they are likely to become your clientele.

Newspaper and magazine ads aren't the only form of print

advertising you might want to try. Printed fliers or brochures describing your establishment, location, hours of operation, and menu passed out to local businesses, including motels and inns, car rental agencies, and local theaters, can be effective. So can copies of your menu, placed in the rooms of motels or at the front desk. When using fliers or menus, it's best to try to have them displayed directly in a motel room or have them handed to potential customers along with their rental car keys, rather than being placed in a rack or stacked on a counter in the lobby or at the department of tourism. This isn't always possible, of course. A few menus pinned to community or tourist bulletin boards is an inexpensive and often effective advertising method, too.

The Yellow Pages of your telephone directory are another good source of inexpensive advertising. You can choose to have a display ad, available in varying sizes at a range of costs, or a simple listing at a much cheaper cost. In addition to being a good source of advertising, it's a service to customers. Sometimes people don't quite remember the name of a restaurant or just which town it's located in. When they turn to the Yellow Pages, their memories are jogged. Sometimes people are looking for a restaurant in a specific town, not having a particular one in mind, and if they see your name there, you may garner new custom.

Another method of advertising combines community involvement with self-interest. Most communities have various fund-raising functions that you can help sponsor. Most high-school and college yearbooks, for example, carry advertising to help offset the cost of printing.

If you live in an area that is rich in cultural events, you may also find that many of these sell ad space in their programs. Community theaters take advertising in their programs. Usually the costs for such ads and sponsorships are fairly small and the goodwill you generate can be considerable.

Radio advertising. An ad heard on the radio can be a very effective and relatively inexpensive selling tool, and a variety of methods for exploiting this medium exist. You can have an ad made up and read over the air. An announcer generally reads the ad, and if he or she has firsthand knowledge of your place, often adds comments. Anytime you can get someone to endorse you personally, the better.

You can also sponsor a segment of a program, such as the weather or sports news. Before or after the segment your restaurant is mentioned as a supporter, often with a few spoken lines describing your establishment. Public radio doesn't take direct advertising, but you can often reach a significant audience by underwriting a portion of a program that you think would appeal to your potential clientele.

Before deciding on the particular radio station to use, do a little research. What kind of clientele are you trying to reach? If yours is an up-market restaurant, you might find that public radio, which attracts educated and moneyed listeners, is the place for you. If yours is a casual and trendy joint, you might want to try a progressive music or jazz station.

Wherever on the dial you decide your market lies, get some information from the station before going any further. Most stations have a demographic breakdown of their audience for the advertisers. Call or ask for it in writing as well as for their rate schedule.

Many radio stations have facilities in their advertising departments to prepare ads. They have copywriters and the announcers often make the tapes. Such departments are a good place to start. You may well want to prepare your own copy, particularly if you are good at writing, and submit it to them for them to read. You may also want to give them ideas, preferring to let them do most of the work of writing selling copy. If you do this, be sure to retain the right of consultation before allowing anything on the air.

You may be tempted to read your ad yourself on the air. Be wary of this unless you have experience in public speaking. It's usually better to let professionals do the talking.

The time of day when an ad runs also contributes to or detracts from its success. If you feature a luncheon special, make sure it runs in the morning and through to lunchtime. If you choose a station that plays in offices, make sure to have your ads run weekdays during working hours. If you wish to draw a sophisticated evening clientele, advertise on a classical station in the late afternoon and evening.

Television advertising. An alternative to the spot radio ad is television advertising. TV advertising is generally quite expensive, and very tricky to do well. Unless you have a lot of money to spend on getting a professional ad made, television restaurant ads tend to look amateurish. The art of filming real interiors is difficult and very specialized. The same is true with shooting food.

You also have to hire professional actors unless you want to risk amateur and silly performances. Should you for one reason or another decide to do your own ads, be sure to get professional coaching. Few of us want to appear like the manic people doing their own car ads. The temptation can be great —you are a great host, you love people, maybe you had the lead in your high-school musical. But think twice, and then consider what Kenny Merlino of Hot Diggity used to say (at least half seriously). He said that if he ever decided to do his own ads, he should be sacked.

The above warning against television notwithstanding, there is one inexpensive method of getting your name on television that will not embarrass you or your customers. This is the method of donating to television auctions or charity drives. This usually takes the form of contributing meals awarded when someone pledges a certain amount of money. You can also contribute money to a televised fund drive. Whichever method is used, your name and address are read on the air. Sometimes the announcers will add a word or two of endorsement as well.

Assessing the value of advertising. When preparing to spend money for any ad, you will naturally be concerned about the cost versus the success. It can be difficult to judge the success of an ad when you're trying to get your name known for the first time. However, once your ads have run awhile, you can begin to assess their worth.

Ask customers how they found out about you. You might also try using a coupon in any print ad you run that is redeemable for a discount on an item or meal, free drink, or dessert. Place the ad in two papers or magazines with a code differentiating one from the other. The kind of response you get from this approach will be direct, telling you which paper or magazine draws better.

In general, for an ad to be considered successful, it should draw business of at least 10 percent more than its cost. In the beginning it may be difficult to assess this, but after a while you will be able to tell which ads draw well, which ones don't, and why. You may wish to run some ads to keep your name in the forefront of people's minds, even if they don't draw particularly well. These include those that are inexpensive, such as a small ad in a local newspaper or one supporting a good cause, such as a community event.

The owner of Junell's Restaurant and Catering of Redding, California, includes an advertising budget in their operating expenses. Junell Gill, co-owner of the business along with her son Scott and daughter Melissa Gill-Anderson, concentrates efforts on donating to charitable events and buying newspaper ads. They also use radio advertising.

Like many others, however, they report that the best advertising is the word-of-mouth referrals that come from providing good food and service and treating customers with the utmost care. No matter how good your advertising, the best method of creating loyal customers is to treat them well.

As stressed throughout this book, the better the value you can provide your customers in the way of serving a need, providing good food and service, sound management, and an overall pleasant experience by setting high standards and being attentive to details, the better a restaurant you will create. The better the restaurant, the more loyal the clientele and the bigger the chance for success—once the word gets around.

A Closing Note

Most of us who are interested in food have at least toyed with the dream of running our own show. And that's what a successful restaurant is, a different show each night or mealtime.

In the twelve chapters of this book, I have discussed methods for planning a successful restaurant. Throughout, I have touched on the areas of utmost importance in restaurant planning. But in closing, it's worth reiterating what I've come to regard as the ten most critical steps in starting a restaurant.

1. Start by looking inward at your reasons for starting a restaurant; then develop your concept as a reflection of yourself.
2. Begin examining the feasibility of your plan by determining a market and a locale for your business.
3. Create a business plan, including profit projections and structure, which will help define the needs of the business to make it successful.
4. Secure financing, making your business legal and safe.
5. Plan carefully the heart of the business, the food and beverages to be served, and how to acquire them.
6. Find the right space (in the right location) for your restaurant.
7. Make the chosen space your own through smart decisions in renovating or building.
8. Lay out and furnish the restaurant, from the kitchen through the dining room, with an eye to utility as well as decor.

9. Hire the best staff you can and manage them well.
10. Let the world know that your new restaurant will soon, or does now, exist.

Three more points cry out for repeating here, too; they are the major pitfalls in the restaurant business, as determined by the Small Business Administration. The SBA says that most restaurants fail because of undercapitalization, lack of management skills, and disagreements among partners. By considering the potential for these problems up front, I hope you will be armed with at least a preliminary understanding of what it takes to open a successful restaurant.

As you have surely gathered by now, starting a restaurant is not for the unenterprising who look for an easy way to make a comfortable living. It is for people with a creative drive and business sense who can determine a community's need and capitalize upon it.

It is for people with good organizational skills, who enjoy people, love food, and have a love of theater. For these people the restaurant business can bring immense satisfaction.

The desire to satisfy and please others through food, service, and even a little fantasy can have an elemental draw that becomes an integral part of the restaurateur—as the many people mentioned in this book can attest.

Index